RETURN TO GAN

Second edition
Published in 2001 by
WOODFIELD PUBLISHING
Bognor Regis, West Sussex PO21 5EL, UK

© Michael Butler, 2001

ISBN 0 873203 52 7

RAF Gan 1960: NAAFI break at CCS/Receiver station by WO Marsh's garden.

Return to Gan

An illustrated diary
1960 & 1998

M<small>ICHAEL</small> B<small>UTLER</small>

Woodfield Publishing
~WEST SUSSEX • ENGLAND ~

RAF Gan 1960 looking towards Feydhoo.

RAF Gan 1960 looking towards the Gan Channel and Viligili.

Contents

RAF Gan. CCS & Receiver Station. 1960.

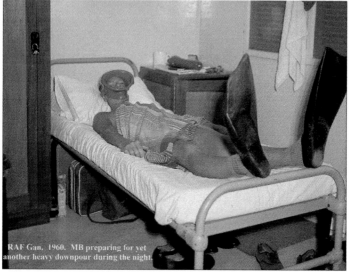

RAF Gan. 1960. MB preparing for yet another heavy downpour during the night.

6 · RETURN TO GAN

Acknowledgements

To my wife, Diane, for agreeing to take on the task of correcting my rotten English and getting the punctuation correct as well as her patience with me when trying to book a time-slot on our PC.

To our offspring Simon and Louise for their great patience in trying to show Dad just how it should be done when it came to operating with new software packages. Just as well they have both been away at university for much of the time I was writing this.

To Stan Seal for providing me with the copy of the RAFA *Air Mail* publication when I was in hospital which revived my interest in Gan and has led to the writing of this document.

To Charles Hampton, my great friend and mentor of some forty years, for his continued support and encouragement.

To Russ Wickson the former Archivist of the RAF Changi Association who provided me with historic information on the RAF and their association with the Maldives and for agreeing to read through the initial draft of the document to provide me with feedback.

To Ravi Patel of Kodak, a great family friend, for organising the contacts for transparency copying onto Photo CD through a Professional Service Bureau.

To Ashwin Shah and Linda Watling of Myriad Audio Visual Sales Ltd who had the task of transferring my ageing transparencies onto compact disc and for organising software backup support with Kodak.

To Jack (Buster) Ansell for the provision of detailed maps of the Maldives and of the Addoo Atoll in particular. These have provided me with the correct spellings for Maldive Atolls and Islands and also the base information for my Addoo Atoll outline sketch in the document.

To John Hunting, ex RAF Ganite, 1967-1968 for information on the Swimming Pagar.

To Philippa Roberts for proof reading and correcting my draft document.

To Jack (John) Findlay for being a friend, colleague, drinking partner and my Radio Gan controller over the months we were both serving the RAF on Gan. Additional thanks to Jack for shinning up some of the aerial masts with my camera and taking a number of the panoramic photographs which appear in this book.

I will buy the next round!

RAF Gan. 1960. Mike Butler & Jack Findlay.

Foreword

What I have tried to do in the following pages is to provide an overview of my and my colleagues' lives on Gan with the RAF in the year 1960. I have attempted to do this in the form of an illustrated diary using information extracted from many of the letters I sent home during that year as a basis for my words.

The photographs I took during my time on Gan, in the form of transparencies, have been digitised by Kodak and transferred to a compact disc. I have selectively enlarged and computer enhanced many of these to help illustrate the diary.

How successful I have been in doing this I will leave for you to judge. Trying to recall, in detail, events that occurred some 37 years ago, has not always been easy.

These are my words and pictures and I have not, with intent, tried to offend anyone. It is how I remember events from that time. If you know I have got it wrong then I apologise in advance. If you are aware of the true story then please let me know.

After I had started to record events from 1960 in this diary, my wife and I became aware that the Travel Operator Kuoni were offering package tours to the Maldives which included Gan. We booked a ten-day holiday and returned to Gan in October 1998. What we found during our ten days in the Addoo Atoll and on Gan in particular is recorded in the latter part of this book. It was a fascinating visit which we think will appeal to many ex-RAF 'Ganites' as well as those seeking to get away from it all.

It should be noted that Kuoni are no longer marketing package holidays to Gan. However, the travel company Elite Vacations is advertising all year round inclusive packages to the island via Male. The hotel complex on Gan is now called 'Equator Village' and details of the holidays can be found in the *Elite Vacations 2001* holiday brochure.

Mike Butler
April 2001

RAF Gan 1960. The Jetty.

1960. *The Jetty (above); NAAFI Club Terrace (below).*

New NAAFI seating area. RAF Gan. January 1960

Introduction

It was early in May 1957 that I received the first indication that the deferral of my National Service was coming to an end. I had joined my employers, International Aeradio Limited (IAL) straight from school in 1951 as a trainee and one day a week I attended Watford Technical College in order to obtain a National Certificate in Electrical Engineering.

On attaining the age of 18 years, in 1954, I became eligible for National Service, but because I was studying, my employer obtained a deferral for me so I could continue my studies.

In May 1957 I received a warrant from the Ministry of Labour and National Service informing me that on 15th May I was to submit myself for medical examination at the Medical Board Centre in St Albans. This I did, and was told that I was "A1 and fit for anything". I was asked if I had a preference as to the service in which I would like to serve and I answered "The Royal Air Force" as it was the most relevant to my work experience at that time. IAL had been awarded a contract from the Ministry of Defence to design, develop and manufacture a Communications Control System for the RAF and at this time I was working in the development laboratories and was deeply involved with this contract.

Due to my continuing studies, I did not receive my call-up letter from the Ministry of Labour and National Service until 1959. When it came, it said that I was to report to No.2 Reception Unit at RAF Cardington, Bedford for my two-year enlistment.

The RAF personnel associated with the CCS contract were well aware that I was due to commence my National Service. Since the first batch of equipment had now been manufactured and was to be installed at RAF Gan in the Maldive Islands, they thought it would be logical for me to go and assist in the installation, commissioning and operation, so wheels were put in motion within the RAF for this to happen.

I was told that I would have to do the mandatory initial training (square bashing) and that arrangements would then be made for me to take a trade test as soon as possible after reporting for service. It was also suggested that I would have to attend a short training course at an RAF station in order to designate my trade. I could not believe that all this was going to happen to me: *a National Serviceman!*

From Cardington I was sent to the Recruit Training Wing at RAF Bridgnorth for initial training. In my second week I was told to report to RAF Locking, near Weston-super-Mare, for a trade test. I came away from Locking after a day with the dizzy rank of Junior Technician (J/T). Initial training then continued and I was very glad when it was all over!

From Bridgnorth I was posted to the RAF Radio Training School at Compton Bassett for a familiarisation course on ground radio equipment. This course lasted about six weeks after which I was officially known as a "Ground Wireless Fitter."

In my last week of training at Compton Bassett my posting came through. It was, indeed, to RAF Gan and I was instructed to travel to RAF Lyneham on Wednesday 16th December for a flight out the following day.

I counted myself very fortunate to be in this situation, and wondered just what the next 12 months would bring...

RAF Gan 1960. The "Ganade" drinks factory.

RAF Gan 1960

RAF Gan 1960. British Forces Post Office 180.

RAF Hithadhoo. 1960. Aircraft Radio Beacon Masts.

RAF Gan. Comms Section Crew. "The Vikings". Dhoni Racing. Boxing Day. 1959.

1960. Maldivians make their way home in the evening via the causeway.

21-12-1959   RAF Laundry. Katunayake, Ceylon.

20-12-1959   RAF Katunayake. Ceylon. 243 Transit Billets.

16 · RETURN TO GAN

Getting there

The Flight to Ceylon

We left Lyneham at about 10:00hrs on Thursday 17th December 1959 on an RAF de Haviland Comet. The first stop was at Nicosia, Cyprus for refuelling. We landed at around 15:00hrs British time, 17:00hrs local time. There were, apparently, two very senior officers on board, and consequently over France and until landing at Nicosia we were escorted by four jet fighter aircraft (type and make unknown). Lunch and tea were served on board and came pre-packed in cardboard boxes.

While refuelling was being carried out at Nicosia we were taken to the airport lounge. Here you could buy *"Velly nice tinkets"* (at a velly high price!). Even postcards were one shilling each – only 5p in today's money but very expensive at that time.

Nicosia, what one could see of it, seemed very brown and quite barren. It was not very hot and just beginning to get dark. My RAF greatcoat was needed for the walk back to the plane. We left Nicosia about one and a half-hours after landing en route now for Karachi.

The flying time to Karachi was about five hours and it was, of course, dark all the way. The first signs of Karachi were its lights, quite a sight from the air. We landed at 03:00hrs in the middle of the night and were taken by bus to a restaurant about half a mile from the airport for breakfast. The meal was served by Pakistanis in traditional dress and consisted of fried eggs, bacon and chips, followed by toast, marmalade and tea. Very good it was too.

We returned to the airport and were once again subjected to the *"Velly nice lace, velly cheap"* routine – even at four in the morning!

We took off from Karachi at about 04:15 local time en route for Katunayake, Ceylon and travelled south along the west coast of India. The sunrise from seven and a half miles up was absolutely beautiful, one of those sights that become indelibly printed in one's mind forever. The West Coast of India is very mountainous in places and many rivers can be seen flowing into the sea. The soil looked very red.

The first sight of Ceylon came about five minutes after leaving the shores of India. Again, what a sight, dozens and dozens of palm trees, paddy fields and little huts dotted amongst the palms. It was a great pity that, for security reasons, we were not allowed to use our cameras.

After landing at Ceylon we were immediately struck by the intense heat and humidity. It flooded into the aircraft the second the doors were opened and wrapped itself around us like a thick, soggy blanket. We had had to travel in our 'best blue' uniforms and what with having to carry two kit bags, a small-pack and greatcoat, we were, to say the very least, warm.

We disembarked and with our kit were taken to the reception room at the airport by bus. Here we were given rupees and cents in exchange for our English pounds – fourteen rupees for twenty-one shillings. Free tea could also be obtained at the airport and this helped to cool us down, even though it was piping hot.

From the airport we were taken to the RAF 'transit billet', which was about a mile from the airport. We were told that we might have to wait up to a week for a plane to Gan. There were already about 30 people waiting to go.

We were all very comfortable in the transit camp and the meals were good. The billets were situated amongst the palm trees which were festooned with large numbers of coconuts. Small lizards called 'chit-chats' could be seen running up and down the billet's rafters and end walls. Large fans kept the place reasonably cool and wickerwork walls helped in allowing the air to circulate.

Our beds were quite comfortable but I could not understand why the bed legs were standing in open-topped Coke and beer cans that had been filled with some kind of liquid. The corporal in charge of our billet soon apprised us of their purpose. There are a considerable number of insects on the loose in Ceylon including scorpions, some rather large spiders and many more besides. The liquid in the cans was paraffin and would, he said, deter "*most* creepy-crawlies" from making their way up the bed legs and into your 'pit'. For this reason we were told never to leave our shoes, or anything else for that matter, on the billet floor but to put everything away in our personal lockers. We were also advised never to walk around with bare feet, and to make sure the insides of our shoes were clear before putting them on, as well as checking under the sheets of our beds before jumping in at night.

The dangers of not following these simple safety procedures, as far as the local insect population was concerned, were amply demonstrated by an incident in our billet on our second afternoon in camp. We were all taking it easy, most of us lying on our beds reading, writing letters or just relaxing. It was during this tranquil situation that somebody first spotted "it" on the billet floor.

"It" was a rather large, brown scorpion taking a constitutional walk up the middle of our billet. All the new and very green airmen, including myself, immediately jumped onto their beds and someone shouted very loudly for the corporal. He duly arrived and soon saw the object of our attention. His words were not very encouraging.

"Oh there's hundreds of those around here," he said, taking a length of cotton out of his pocket. He tied a small noose at one end of the cotton before approaching the scorpion from behind and dangling the noose just above the insect's tail. The noose was raised and lowered a number of times, just touching the tail. This obviously annoyed the scorpion and the tail, complete with sting was raised to make ready for an attack. The cotton noose was then slipped over the erect tail and sting and pulled tight. The nearest fire bucket was then used as the unfortunate creature's final resting-place. We were warned not to take it out of the water for at least seven hours as there was a good chance that if taken out any sooner it would revive. We didn't need telling twice. None of us 'greenhorns' intended to go anywhere near that fire bucket!

Our continuing stay at Katunayake was very pleasant but every evening, just before it got dark, we nearly always had a thunderstorm and an accompanying downpour of rain. The monsoon ditches around the camp were some four feet deep and we soon realised why. They very quickly filled to the top. As night descended the jungle noises would start. Especially after rain, the sound of crickets, frogs, birds and the chattering of the monkeys was at its peak and almost deafening. These noises continued throughout the night at a diminished level and were often supplemented by totally unidentifiable and quite frightening noises coming from the jungle a long way off.

"Could that have been a tiger?" we asked each other, apprehensively. If so, we would need more than a Coke tin filled with paraffin to protect us.

As the sun arose next morning at about 0600 hrs the local 'alarm clock' would go off and your chance of getting any more undisturbed sleep would disappear. The local monkey population that frequented the palms would chase each other through the branches and invariably manage to knock at least one coconut down onto the red tiled roof of the billet. We all came to believe that they did this on purpose. Perhaps they were thinking, "If we are up and looking for breakfast, then why shouldn't you be?" Certainly, nothing could have woken us up more effectively.

On Saturday 19th December, Harry (who was in the next bed to mine in the transit billet) and I decided to hire a bike each from an enterprising local who had set up a bicycle hire business just outside the gates of the camp. The hire charge was the princely sum of three rupees per week, and what a rare selection of bikes he had! Many were obviously very old indeed and others appeared to be locally-assembled 'hybrids'. However, whatever their gender, they all appeared to be well maintained and roadworthy.

The next day we cycled into Negombo, which was not far outside the camp, passing the RAF laundry on our way. All the local children shouted *"ello"* as we passed them and always expected a wave or greeting to be shouted back. The small shacks outside the town and camp entrance were mostly made of dried palm branches plaited together. They all looked a bit rickety to me and certainly not very rainproof.

We slowly became accustomed to the heat and humidity and were beginning to get slightly tanned, but we soon learnt that taking a shower several times a day was essential if you were to avoid 'prickly heat' or other nasty rashes in embarrassing places. Drinking to replace lost fluids was also essential and the NAAFI did a roaring trade in cans of soft drink and beer.

There was still no news as to when we would get a seat on an aircraft out to Gan, although a number of the lads who had arrived before us had now gone. We were becoming resigned to the fact that our Christmas was probably going to be spent at Katunayake and not with the other 400 plus blokes already stationed on Gan.

Off to Gan

At last we heard on 20th December that we should be prepared to leave Ceylon the following day. An Australian Air Force Bristol Freighter was due in en route to Gan and there should be room for six of us.

Harry, who was to work at station HQ, Colin and Dave the two firemen, Trevor the cook and I all got seats and W/O Marsh joined us. He was going to Gan to look after the Communication & Control Section (CCS) and the Receiver station, where I expected to work. The plane duly arrived the next day and was on time.

Flying in a Bristol Freighter, as a passenger, is not something to be repeated too often. Temporary single canvas seats had been fitted down the port side of the aircraft for the six of us and to our immediate right was an enormous packing case. This contained a replacement engine for a Britannia which had become unserviceable (U/S) at Gan. The rest of the aircraft was totally full of packing cases of every size, all, it seemed, destined for Gan. We could now see clearly why only six of us had been given a seat.

The preliminaries performed by the pilot before take off were interesting indeed. We were all strapped into our seats and the aircraft was taxied to the end of the runway. The pilot then gave each engine a full throttle test in turn. The starboard engine sounded fine and healthy, but the port one, which we could see clearly, sounded distinctly sick. Great sheets of flame belched from the exhaust whenever full throttle was attempted and it coughed and spluttered in protest. This engine testing went on for about 10 minutes.

My apprehension, like the rest of my fellow passengers was rising by the minute and we all fully expected the Australian pilot to taxi back to the hardstanding and get the engine looked at, however, this did not happen, which came as a bit of a surprise. He started the aircraft down the runway with the port engine still sounding as if it was about to cough its last and managed to take off. We missed the palms by a whisker and were at last off to Gan.

The engine sounded much sweeter as we gained height. We, on the other hand, felt very much colder as we flew between 2,500 and 3,000 feet. No frills on this aircraft like pressurisation or cabin heating, and what a noisy aircraft the Bristol Freighter was. Conversation was virtually impossible.

After some four hours of noisy flying we were circling around RAF Gan. We looked down with a certain amount of disappointment. Was this 'runway' really going to be our home for the coming year?

The Gan Posting

As soon as our Bristol Freighter touched down on Gan we immediately became aware of the intense heat. It was about 15:30 hrs in the afternoon and the sun was shining brightly. We disembarked, collected our kit and were taken to a reception office in station HQ. The formalities of booking the six of us in were soon over and we airmen were taken to the transit billet at the top end of the island.

This billet was a traditionally-built Maldivian *kadjan*. The building had an earth floor and contained about a dozen beds and personal lockers. The only concession to modernisation was that corrugated iron sheets had replaced the traditional plaited palm leaf roof. We were each given a blanket, a sheet and a Mosquito net.

We were told that we would probably have to stay in the *kadjan* for a couple of nights until a bed was available in one of the new billets.

As I was due to start work at the CCS/Receiver station the next day and the other lads were starting their jobs, we decided to use the rest of the afternoon to cool down by taking a dip in the Indian Ocean. It was just like getting into a warm bath.

All newcomers on Gan were known as 'moonies' and we received the traditional wolf whistles from all and sundry as we entered the sea. I suppose we did look a little anaemic. We were told that the midday temperature on the aircraft pan was 150°F in the sun and shade temperatures were likely be 100°F plus.

In the *kadjan* was the first time that any of us had experienced sleeping under mosquito nets. We all found that it was extremely hot and that getting off to sleep was very difficult. Once asleep it was all too easy to move arms or legs against the mosquito net which was just what the local mosquito population was waiting for. We all woke up next morning with a number of bites. We also all exhibited a rather pink hue due to our exposure to the sun whilst swimming the previous day.

We only had to spend two nights sleeping in the *kadjans* and were then moved into our rooms in the new billets. The billets were roughly allocated to those groups of airmen who worked in a particular section on the camp. The billet that I moved into, number 47, was used by those personnel who worked in the Communications centre and associated sections. I was allocated a bed in room 7, and soon found myself with lads that worked at the CCS/Receiver Station under W/O Marsh.

The three days up to Christmas eve were spent working. In our leisure time the five of us who arrived on the Bristol Freighter tried to meet up whenever possible to explore the island. We would also meet for a drink in the old NAAFI club each evening where we would manage to down the odd 'tinny' (can of beer) or two.

The old NAAFI was housed in one of the locally-built *kadjans* but was shortly to be demolished.

Christmas Eve arrived and the newly-built NAAFI club, just behind the old NAAFI, opened. Everyone celebrated its opening and Christmas by getting very drunk. I have never seen so many legless people in all my life!

The Navy had a destroyer and a cruiser moored in the lagoon and the majority of their crews were in the NAAFI at one time or another, celebrating.

One sailor came reeling over to our billet at about one in the morning. He wanted to know, "Whish way to port?" We pointed him in the direction of the jetty and his ship. That was the last we saw of him. He must have got very wet as it rained heavily nearly all night.

Christmas and Boxing Day were nominated as leave days for most people and a series of events had been arranged to keep everyone entertained. There was a fishing contest, the largest catch in weight winning the top prize. There was also the traditional Christmas Day lunch in the Airmen's Mess, with the Officers serving the airmen, and in the evening there was a barbecue at the NAAFI club.

Boxing Day was similarly organised and the highlight of the day was the *dhoni* boat racing between representatives of the various camp sections.

Dhonis were the locally-built Maldivian boats. They were about 20 feet long with a beam of around five feet and they all had a very distinctive curved prow. The coxswain stood on a raised platform to the aft of the boat to control the helm. It was possible to have up to ten oarsmen, sitting in pairs, along the length of the boat. These boats also had facilities for fitting a mast and sails when there was sufficient wind blowing but these were not allowed in the race.

The RAF's Fire, Marine, Comms, ATC, MT and HQ sections were all represented as well as a boat crewed by some Army lads who were also present on Gan. Boats raced each other in pairs, with the winner going through to the next heat.

The representatives of our Comms section just had to be different from everyone else and dressed up as Vikings, complete with horned helmets. Where they managed to find these items of clothing on Gan one can only guess. Their outfits certainly caused a great deal of amusement during the races but unfortunately they only managed to finish fifth.

Both Christmas and Boxing Day were enjoyed by everyone, everyone that is, that remained sober and was not sleeping off a very large hangover.

All us 'moonies' had spent a great deal of time in the sun watching all the activities going on over the holiday period and as a consequence we had all been sunburnt and skin was now starting to peel. The NAAFI shop only carried supplies of "Nivea Cream" and this had to suffice in relieving the soreness.

In the end, the fishing contest was abandoned due to lack of support and the barbecue at the NAAFI was poorly attended, barbecued sausages being the only items on offer. I would imagine the fact that over the two days of Christmas just over 63,000 cans of beer were consumed, plus gallons of whisky at 4d per nip, may have had something to do with this. (At this time the island population consisted of 400 RAF personnel, 20 Army and on about 85 transiting sailors. For those who do not have access to a calculator this works out at 125 cans of beer per man). So that's where the headache came from... and we thought we'd had too much sun!

RAF Gan. 1960. A DC6 of Eagle Airways delivering freight.

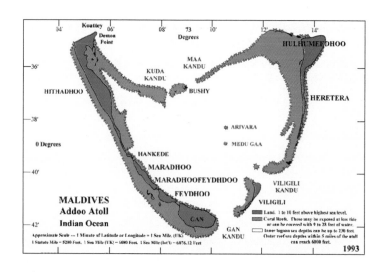

MALDIVES
Addoo Atoll
Indian Ocean

1993

RAF GAN 1960. Sunset.

26 · RETURN TO GAN

The Maldives & the Addoo Atoll

Location

The Addoo Atoll is the southernmost in a chain of atolls that make up the Maldives. Each atoll consists of a number of islands, usually in a horsesoe-shaped group with a natural lagoon at their centre.

Maldives

The Maldives, formerly the Maldive Islands, is an island republic in Southern Asia located in the northern Indian Ocean, south-west of the southern tip of India. Nearly 1,200 small coral islands are contained in 26 major atolls. The total land area is only about 115 square miles. The capital and largest city in the Maldives is Male; its population in 1990 was 55,130.

Land and Resources

All the islands are low-lying and only have very small tracts of arable land. The vegetation is dominated by coconut palms and breadfruit trees and the climate is tropical and very humid. The average annual temperature is 80°F, with little seasonal variation. Average rainfall is 60 inches, most of which falls between May and November. The principal natural resource is the marine life of the surrounding seas but more recently tourism is becoming dominant, especially in the northern islands and provides a lucrative income for Maldivians.

Population

The population of the Maldives, in 1993, was estimated to be 238,363, yielding an average population density of 2,073 persons per square mile. The most populated atolls are those of Male, the capital and principal commercial centre; Suvadiva and Tiladummati. The people are ethnically heterogeneous, incorporating Indian, Sinhalese, Arabian and African elements. Islam is the state religion and nearly all the people are Sunni Muslims. The language is *Divehi*, an Indo-European tongue related to Sinhalese.

Economy & Government

The Maldivian economy is dominated by fishing, which accounts for about 60% of all the export trade. The catch is primarily tuna but corals and shells are also harvested. Coconuts are the principal agricultural product and most food has to be imported. Industrial activity is largely limited to fish processing and the manufacture of garments. The tourist industry is growing and in the late 1980s annual receipts totalled $39 million. The national currency is the *rufiyaa* which is made up of 100 *laari*. (11.7 *rufiyaa* to one US dollar in 1995).

The Maldives is a republic governed under a constitution promulgated in 1968. Executive power is vested in a president, elected every five years by universal adult suffrage. The president appoints a cabinet that is responsible to the unicameral legislative body, the 48-member *Majlis* or Citizens' Council.

History

The islands were settled by Buddhist peoples from southern Asia. Islam was introduced in the 12th century. The Portuguese traded at Male in the latter half of the 15th century. Although the islands were ruled by a local sultan, European influence was established over the area, first by the Dutch in the 17th century and later by the British. In 1887 the Maldives formally became a British protectorate. In 1965 the Maldives achieved independence as a sultanate and in 1968 the people voted to establish a republic.

In 1988, Indian troops were called in to foil a coup attempt by Tamil mercenaries. Since the late 1980s the Maldives has been the focus of concerns that global warming will lead to rising sea levels, the very low elevations of the republic's islands making them particularly vulnerable.

The Island of Gan

Gan is just one of the islands in the Addoo Atoll and is also the last and most southerly island in the Maldives group. It is about 1¾ miles long and ¾ miles wide. It is situated at Longitude 73° 09.3' East of Greenwich, and 0° 41.6' South of the Equator. The runway, which is the most dominant feature of this virtually flat island, is situated at 280°, reciprocal 100°. The 280° approach starts in the sea adjacent to the Gan Channel and ends in the sea at the channel between Gan and Feydhoo.

The runway is 8,700 feet long and is 150 feet wide. Its approach lights at both ends are situated on high level posts and gantries in the sea on the reef.

The Addoo Atoll Geography

There are four main sea channels (*kandus*) into the Addoo Atoll lagoon. These are: the *Gan Kandu*; the *Kuda Kandu*; the *Maa Kandu*; the *Viligili Kandu*. These are all known to be deep water channels, but the one usually used by shipping is the Gan Channel as this affords the easiest, shortest and straightest approach into the lagoon. There are navigational marker buoys in the sea to aid a safe approach.

It is known that during World War 2 that the *Queen Mary*, then being used as a troop carrier, anchored in the Addoo Atoll for a short period, having come in via the Gan Channel.

Once in the lagoon, both large and small vessels need to take great care when moving since there are many uncharted reefs and also two small submerged islands, Arivara and Medu Gaa, in almost the centre of the lagoon need to be avoided.

In 1960 one of the RAF's High Speed Launches used on Search and Rescue missions came to grief on one of these reefs. The launch was estimated to be going at a speed in excess of 40 knots when it hit an unseen and uncharted reef just below the water line. Luckily no one was seriously injured in this accident but the whole of the bottom of the HSL was ripped out and it sank very quickly. Fortunately, it settled onto the top of the reef. This just gave the crew time to radio back to Gan for help and the launch was retrieved later by lashing the boat between two RAF Pinnaces and bringing it back to Gan. It is understood that the boat was eventually put back into service on Gan but its original engines were a total write-off.

Each HS Launch was fitted with two Shackleton aircraft type engines, (Rolls-Royce 2,450hp Griffons), so the cost of replacing these would have been very high.

There are many other sea channels into the lagoon between the islands but the majority of these are comparatively shallow. For example the sea channel between Gan and Feydhoo, at low tide, can be walked across with ease and is little more than waist deep. The Maldivians that used to work on Gan during the day and lived on Feydhoo often used to go home this way, carrying their possessions in bundles on their heads. If they were using this route during the day it was not unusual to see them with an umbrella up, to give them some shade, even though they were up to their chests in water. A most memorable sight. The old causeway between the two islands was unusable for traffic, so lorries and other heavy vehicles also used this watery route to get between the islands.

The islands in the Addoo Atoll, going in a clockwise direction from Gan are: Gan, Feydhoo, Maradhoofeydhoo, Maradhoo, Hankede, Hithadhoo; then comes the *Kuda Kandu (Channel)*, followed by: three minor small islands, including Bushy, and the *Maa Kandu (Channel)*. Next is the island of Hulhumeedhoo and Heretera, then comes the *Viligili Kandu (Channel)*, followed by the island of Viligili, the *Gan Kanda (Channel)*, and back again to Gan.

Before the RAF came to Gan to establish it as a flying staging post in 1956, the island was thickly wooded as are the majority of the larger islands in the Addoo Atoll. Gan was also inhabited by a small number of Maldivians. It is understood that the agreement between the British and Maldivian Governments was that Maldivians displaced by the RAF would be re-housed by the MOD on a neighbouring island of their choice.

The MOD, through the AMWD, arranged for prefabricated houses to be manufactured in the UK for such displaced locals and then shipped for assembly on the appropriate island in the Atoll. Many of the original residents of Gan opted for a move to Feydhoo, especially when they were told that eventually some would be required to work for the RAF whilst the island was being changed into its new role as a staging post.

Many locals were employed by the AMWD during the construction of all the buildings and facilities required. The AMWD also brought in many Pakistani workers to supplement the work force. The Pakistani living quarters, together with a suitable canteen and all support services was established at the north western end of Gan.

It was very important that Gan had a fresh water supply laid on to meet the heavy demands placed on it by the resident RAF contingent as well as the AMWD staff, workers and locals during their time on the island. Boreholes were sunk at the centre of the island and the pumping station has since been able to fully meet the demand for water.

Hithadhoo was thickly wooded and had only been cleared at its southern end for the RAF's Transmitter buildings and Aerial Farms. Hithadhoo already had a freshwater well, established before the RAF arrived. Hithadhoo also sported some of the largest land crabs that one can imagine. All RAF personnel were told to treat them with great respect. At the northern end of Hithadhoo is a small saltwater lake and at its centre a large freshwater lake.

The island of Hulhumeedhoo and Heretera appears to be a major one in the Atoll as far as the local population is concerned. At its northern end is a long-established cemetery and many local people live on this island. Heretera also has a fresh water lake as well as a number of brackish pools. Viligili was uninhabited but sometimes used as a base for local fishing expeditions.

Old NAAFI, RAF Gan, December 1959.

RAF Gan, 1960. Billet number 47.

1960: Gan and Friends

Everyone welcomed in the New Year with the usual display of unbridled enthusiasm, eating and drinking far too much. We had not been on Gan very many days yet but were rapidly changing from 'moonies' to fairly well-tanned locals. We also learnt that in the December just passed, the total rainfall had been 8¼ inches (210 mm) with 4½ inches (114 mm) falling overnight on Christmas and Boxing Day.

From mid-December 1959 there had been no camp Barber and most airmen on the island early in the New Year were looking more like hippies every day. This situation was relieved when a new Pakistani barber, employed by the NAAFI, arrived on 6th January. He worked well into each evening, snipping and clipping all us longhaired louts. For this pleasure he charged 1/6d a cut.

Food in the Airmen's Mess was adequate, if not very exciting. Anti-malarial tablets and salt tablets were put out on the tables for our use. We were advised that we should take the anti-malarial tablets (Paludrine) each day due to the very large number of mosquitoes about. I seem to recall we did this for about the first six weeks then could not be bothered with them. No one suffered from malaria as a result. The salt tablets made you feel sick, so these were given a miss also.

We all had to be fairly diplomatic in what we said about the food as we still had a drink, most evenings, with Trevor the cook who had travelled out on the Bristol Freighter with us and now worked in the Airmen's Mess. One thing we all agreed on was the state of the eggs that were served. It did not matter if they were fried, poached, boiled or scrambled, they tasted foul. Trevor informed us that eggs usually took about four months to reach Gan and therefore had to be sent in a preservative. It was this that made them taste so revolting. He said that he never ate them, and from then on neither did we.

Sunrise on Gan came at 05:45hrs and sunset around 18:00hrs. There was very little twilight after the sun disappeared over the horizon but the high daytime temperatures dropped by just a few degrees. Some of the sunsets on Gan were real 'chocolate box' pictures and many evenings were spent with the camera sitting on a tripod waiting for just the right moment to release the shutter.

It was part of the station's standing orders that trousers must be worn at night as well as socks and shoes if you were going out from your billet. This was an extremely sensible rule and helped prevent the local mosquito population from finding a meal each evening. It was also sensible to wear long-sleeved shirts for the same reason.

The Wildlife

Gan had a very large and active animal and insect population, apart from the mosquitoes. Large flying beetles, some 2 inches long and about ¾ inch in diameter, would hurl themselves at any bright light once it was dark. They could be heard hitting the outside billet and building lights every few minutes and would invariably land up on the ground with their feet in the air. They would usually remain like this, as they seemed to find it almost impossible to right themselves, once inverted.

There were also hundreds of frogs of many different species and size in the swampy area of land in the centre of Gan and they would set up a chorus of calls each evening that could be heard throughout the island. When it rained the noise they made increased considerably in volume. We all knew what *they* were up to! Luckily very few came close enough to the billets to disturb an otherwise good night's sleep.

Every evening about 15 minutes before sunset the resident 'flying foxes' (fruit bats) would return from gorging themselves on the neighbouring islands near to Gan and roost in the few remaining palm trees on the island. It always appeared to us that their return and gathering in the palm branches was very much like a clandestine meeting of the Ku-Klux-Klan. There always seemed to be a considerable noise generated by them as arguments broke out as to whose branch it was, before they settled down for the night.

There was no need to have a watch with you if you went in swimming in the late afternoon, the returning fruit bats would remind you that there was only about a quarter hour of daylight left. We nicknamed them the 'Duty Bat Squadron'.

There were some snakes to be found on Gan, but these were confined to the 500 square yards of thick swampy undergrowth roughly in the centre of the island. This area was gradually being cleared by a Pakistani and Maldivian task force and sprayed regularly by the AMWD Hygiene department to keep down the mosquito population.

The bird population (feathered variety, alas!) was strictly limited on Gan and I can only recall two different types. There were herons, who had 'never had it so good' due to the rich pickings of fish to be had in the shallow sea areas between and around the islands, and also white terns (*Cygis alba*). These birds have forked tails and straight, sharp bills. They are about 10 inches long and have a wingspan of some 22 inches. There was quite a large population of these rather aggressive birds on all the islands in the Addoo Atoll and if you happened to go into an area where eggs had been laid, you would invariably be dive-bombed by the breeding pairs. The white, or 'fairy' tern inhabits many tropical islands around the world and incubates its single egg on a bare branch or in the fork of a tree, with no nest.

Why is it that *tropical* spiders are always so much larger than those commonly found in the UK? Those found on Gan were certainly no exception and although most were not poisonous, you just could not ignore them due to their large size. I recall one of the Maldivians, who worked at the CCS/Receiver station, catching a very large spider in one of the outbuildings. Its body, with legs extended, would easily have covered a saucer. What made it look even more sinister was the fact that it was covered in long black hairs. Our Sergeant decided that he was going to take it back to the billets that evening and, as he put it, "have a bit of fun". Some unsuspecting body was going to have quite a surprise finding it in his bed. We understood that he did not carry out his threat but shipped the spider off to the Natural History Museum in London for identification. Apparently the Sergeant, through a prior arrangement, sent many insects back to the NHM for species identification and classification.

Off to Work

The journey to the CCS/Receiver building, when we first arrived on the island, was usually made each day in the back of an open 10-ton truck. Although bench seats were provided down each side of the truck, sitting on them could be extremely uncomfortable as the drivers seemed to take great delight in going as fast as they could and finding all the potholes that existed in the roads. W/O Marsh threatened one driver that he would have him charged if he "ever drove like that again", after a particularly hair raising journey.

The Maldivians who also worked at the CCS/Receiver building, when offered a lift, were always very selective about which drivers they would travel with, often preferring to walk to or from the building rather than risk their necks in the back of the lorry. The truck used to pick up both day staff and the watch crew outside the Sergeants' mess and we used to travel to the CCS building along the road that passed adjacent to the swampy area of ground near the centre of the island.

At night, at certain times of the year, there seemed to be a population explosion amongst the Gan land snails. These snails were very large. Their shells were between five and six inches in length and about two inches in diameter. The snails certainly seemed to have a death wish and at times would totally cover the road adjacent to the swampy area of land from which they had just emerged. Where they were going is hard to guess.

Some of the MT section drivers seemed to take great delight in seeing how many snails they could squash by weaving back and forth across the road. However this did not seem to make any difference to the snail population and the next night the road would once again be totally covered in these creatures. The sound of crunching shells under the tyres had to be heard to be believed. These snails then seemed to totally disappear for a few months before suddenly re-appearing to embark again on their fateful mission across the highway. When bicycles were issued to all, we were relieved that we could at last take charge of our own and the snails' destinies.

JANUARY

The month of January for those of us from the December 'moonie' contingent was a time of work although in our leisure periods, we managed a bit of island exploration.

I was working with a civilian guy named Alex Cameron of AT&E at the CCS and Receiver station. I had met Alex before being called up to do my National Service, whilst working for IAL. On Gan we worked well together on some channelling equipment which was new to me, and I found the work both interesting and challenging.

All daily CCS/Receiver station staff worked a 4½ day week. Work times were 07:00 hrs to 11:45 hrs and 12:45 hrs to 16:00 hrs, Monday to Friday. The half day off per week could be taken on any day during the week but was usually taken on a Wednesday. There was no work at the weekend.

The other lads I had travelled out to Gan with were all at their new jobs. Harry worked in the Station HQ as a typist and kept us up to date with impending station developments. Brian worked in station Aircraft Servicing; Dave and John worked in the Accounts section; Colin and Tony were Firemen and would keep us up to date on the mail situation. We certainly had blokes in all the right places to keep us informed of just what was happening, or was about to happen.

All the RAF personnel on Gan were paid every fortnight on a Thursday. You did not have to accept all your pay in one lump sum, but could specify just how much you required to carry you over to the next pay day within your pay limit. In this way you could save money quite easily and you knew that the money was secure and available for an emergency.

Room Boys

Not long after becoming settled into our new billet we were approached by some young Maldivian lads who wished to know if they could work for us as our 'room boys'. For the sum of 1/6 per week, each airman could have the luxury of having his own Maldivian room boy. For this sum your room boy would make your bed, wash and iron your civvy clothes, keep your bed space clean and polish your shoes.

We all took up their offer and the new room boys started to work for us the following morning. What luxury, having your own servant!

One shilling and sixpence may not sound very much for performing all these tasks but it was the agreed rate set by the Maldivian Government representative in consultation with the RAF. It should also be remembered that most room boys had at least five airmen that they looked after and some of the more enterprising ones had up to ten.

Most of the room boys were very loyal to the airmen that they worked for and would try to supplement their income by playing cards for money. They were all very skilled at this and would nearly always win. Their skill at cards was always better than mine and so I did not play very often.

Many of the airmen supplemented the 1/6 per week by giving the boys extra chores. Going to the bedding store at the appropriate time and collecting clean sheets was just one of the extra tasks that they were willing to do.

The income they received represented a small fortune to them and they often asked us to buy items at the NAAFI shop. We were always very pleased to do this. Most of the room boys were aged between 8 and 13 and usually travelled to Gan with their friends or relatives who also worked on the island.

It was always a sad occasion for a room boy when someone he had served faithfully finished his tour and returned to the UK or to another overseas posting, but of course, there was always a 'moonie' coming in to replace him.

Mohammed was my room boy and he stayed with me for all of my tour on Gan.

Until employing Mohammed, I had had to wash all my civvy clothes myself. This task was made even harder by the fact that we had no hot water in the billet washrooms and no one seemed able to tell us when we would. Luckily, our 'all-forces KD' (khaki drill) kit was washed at the camp laundry and of course they had hot water by the bucket load.

Mohammed certainly had his work cut out in trying to get my civvy shirts to look clean.

Exploring Gan

In our leisure time, Harry and I spent many hours trudging around Gan, exploring the flora and fauna and at low tide walking out onto the outer reef. What interesting walks these were. When the tide was out, about ¾ mile of the outer reef on the south western side of the island was only under six to eight inches of water and it was easy to walk providing you had some form of protective footwear. If you did not, then you would soon have badly cut feet from all the sharp edges of the coral. Walking on the reef was like walking on broken china with large and small pieces of coral everywhere broken by the heavy seas.

Near to the shore there were dozens of black crabs, not very big, about four to five inches across. They could be seen running up and down the old decaying roots and trunks of palm trees discarded from the island. Walking further towards the reef edge brought you into very shallow and noticeably warmer water, where nothing appeared to live. About two-thirds of the distance to the reef edge were hundreds of large pools, full of fish of all the colours of the rainbow, a really wonderful sight. Just a little further out were dozens and dozens of brittle star fish. There were so many that it was impossible to walk without treading on them. Their bodies were about the size of an old penny and they had five hairy and spidery legs.

Between the starfish and the breakers on the reef edge were a large number of eels, each about 1 foot 6 inches long. These were joined by sea slugs, or as they are more commonly known, 'sea cucumbers'. These really were revolting looking things. They were some five to seven inches long, 1½ inches in diameter and dirty brown in colour. If you had the misfortune to step on one of these creatures it would discharge sticky filaments of its respiratory system from an end orifice, apparently designed to entangle and discourage predators. It certainly was not very nice. The Brown Sea Cucumber is classified as *Thyrone briareus*.

It was possible to get to about 30 feet from the edge of the reef, but here the water was too rough to proceed any further. At this point there were real heavy breakers, some 15 to 20 feet high, where the Indian Ocean impinged directly on the reef edge which then descended almost vertically, some 200 fathoms (1,200 feet) to the seabed below.

On one of our early trips around the island I saw what I thought was an old boat wreck, out on the edge of the reef, possibly from World War II. When we investigated further, by walking out to it, we found the wreck to be that of a Bulldozer! Its driver had apparently been using it to clear uprooted palm trees from the reef but had been caught by the tide and failed to start its engine in time. This must have been quite a hazardous task. He not only had the tide and heavy breakers to contend with; the outer edge of the reef at this point drops away almost vertically, like a cliff edge.

Swimming

It very quickly became obvious that if I was going to enjoy snorkelling over the living coral reefs all around Gan then to be able to swim was an absolute must, but like a number of my colleagues in the RAF, I could not swim. My early attempts to swim had been at school in the late 1940s and early 1950s. These attempts took place at an open-air pool in the UK at the Churchill baths,

Hemel Hempstead. The one thing I remember about the lessons we were forced to take each week from Easter until the end of the summer school term, was the very cold water and being made to put our heads underwater and mentally count to ten before surfacing again. I absolutely hated it and it was not at all conducive to learning.

Now here I was on Gan with seas all around the island at the temperature of a warm bath. Harry was my first teacher and he soon had me doing a few yards breaststroke and diving down a few feet, with eyes open, to retrieve a beer can. All those years of school swimming lessons and fear of the water soon disappeared and my confidence grew daily.

By mid-January and my swimming was coming on well. One of the boys in the billet lent me his face-mask and flippers and Harry and I went for my first look at the coral reef just off the beach by the Officers' Mess on the lagoon side of the island.

It was low tide when we arrived and there was only about 2 feet of water above the coral heads. The stag and branch coral grows some two to three feet high. The growing part of the coral was brown, not white as I had expected, with the tips of each branch almost fluorescent blue. What a sight it was! It was like entering a completely different world of large coral trees with valleys and rock-like formations everywhere which looked like miniature mountains.

The fish, oh, the fish, there were hundreds of them, every colour and shape you could possibly imagine, all swimming in and out of the coral trees. It really was a wonderland. In the coral there were deep narrow channels and it was these that were the most interesting. Each was the oceanic equivalent of Oxford Street in the rush hour with brilliantly coloured fish swimming in all directions. Words are totally inadequate to do justice to such a beautiful sight. It just has to be seen.

The waves that broke on the beach, on the lagoon side of the island, near to where we swam and snorkelled were always very small and very little damage occurred to the living coral city in this area. Just off the beach on the sandy floor, near the coral channels, sea snakes could always be found. These were only about six inches long and looked harmless enough, but if provoked they could give quite a nasty bite. On the rocks amongst the coral were brilliantly coloured clams, vivid blues and greens. These would immediately shut if you touched or went near to them and would send out a jet of water. There were many holes in the smaller rocks and these were the home of bright red sea anemones. They really were beautiful and would retract gracefully as you approached them.

My first visit to the coral reef far exceeded my expectations and, like the view of the sunrise over India that I saw from the plane, will always be imprinted on my mind. After that, whenever the opportunity arose I would don mask and flippers and go off to explore the reef. Every visit was just as magical.

One day I discovered that it was all too easy to be lulled into a sense of false security when snorkelling. No external sounds, only the crackling sound of the coral transmitted to your ears through the water, fish looking for a tasty morsel to eat and the gentle wave motion. With the warm water all around me, what could be more tranquil?

Then, suddenly, I was face to face with a 'monster of the deep'. I had been looking in crevices in the coral channels and realised that about two feet in front of my face mask there was something staring back at me. It was a Moray eel, a very large Moray eel, showing me a perfectly formed set of needle sharp teeth. I backed gently away and as I did so it emerged fully from what I later learnt was its regular resting-place and home. The Moray was some six feet in length and swam off like a sidewinder snake, at high speed, obviously very annoyed at being disturbed. These eels can inflict a very nasty bite and have to be treated with great respect.

I returned to this area of the reef a number of times after that, and quite often the Moray was at home.

During other trips to the reef we saw barracuda, giant manta rays, stingrays, octopus and giant clams. The giant manta rays were really awe-inspiring, like sitting at the end of a runway and having a Victor or Valiant bomber taking off over the top of you but without all the noise. All these creatures were treated with great respect, after all, we were invading aliens in their beautiful world.

The boys from the billet were fishing from the jetty one day and managed to catch a five-foot long shark. It took them over two hours to land it. This was yet another timely reminder of just what dangers were lurking out beyond the reef.

Harry and I spent most weekends snorkelling. We both looked like Red Indians and were at last getting tanned rathe than burnt.

The Runway

After Christmas and New Year the weather was particularly hot and sunny. It was thought that this contributed to major problems with the runway, which had to be closed. Large holes and cracks had appeared and necessitated urgent repairs. It took some two days to effect these repairs. Poor quality cement was thought to be the most likely cause of the problems. This caused yet another delay in the arrival of our mail, which was invariably held up somewhere, usually by an aircraft becoming unserviceable.

Hithadhoo

The island of Hithadhoo in the Addoo Atoll is about seven miles from Gan and it took about 45 minutes to reach it by RAF Pinnace. I first visited Hithadhoo on Monday 11 January and was on the island for only one hour. The water over the reef just off Hithadhoo is very shallow and extends a long way into the lagoon, so a jetty almost a quarter of a mile long had to be built to allow easy access to the island from the RAF's boats. It took some 15 minutes to walk the length of this rather rickety construction.

I was now working on Hithadhoo at the Transmitter station on a fairly regular daily basis. Our working party would leave Gan at 07:00 hrs on the Pinnace and reach Hithadhoo at 07:45 hrs. We would work until 13:15 hrs and then return to Gan. The rest of the day was ours. This trip was always interesting, as we would normally be joined on our boat trip by a number of dolphins for virtually the whole journey to Hithadhoo. They would swim just in front of the bow of the boat and seemed to thoroughly enjoy the experience.

How they had the energy to keep this up for nearly 40 minutes I will never know. They really are delightful and intelligent creatures.

It was whilst I was on Hithadhoo one day, waiting for the boat to take me back to Gan, that I found myself with sufficient time to climb to the 200 foot platform of one of the 250ft aircraft radio beacon masts. What a view there was from this elevated position. You could see all the Addoo Atoll islands at one time. Unfortunately I did not have my camera with me. I promised myself that I would go back again with my camera, but of course I did not get the opportunity.

The Maldivian Way

During my trips to Hithadhoo I met and saw many of the Maldivians who lived on the island. It was always intriguing to see how they coped with the daily problems of living an island existence.

Take the simple task of cleaning your teeth. We just pick up a toothbrush, squeeze on some toothpaste, brush our teeth and rinse with water from the tap. Maldivians living on these islands did not have a toothbrush, toothpaste or water on tap, nevertheless, cleaning their teeth was just as simple for them. First, wet hands in sea, then place fingers in the coral sand, put into mouth and clean teeth and finally, rinse mouth with sea water. I imagine the process must be rather like cleaning your teeth with sandpaper, but all their teeth looked clean and healthy.

Their simple but very efficient approach to living also extended to the task of fishing. They would secure a net at the end of four very long poles, which would then be lowered over the side of a *dhoni*. The poles would be slowly hauled in by two of the fishermen and there would be the fish, dozens of them trapped in the net.

Weather

The end of our first full month on Gan was fast approaching. The weather throughout January had been mainly hot and sunny, but on the 27th there were very strong winds and heavy breakers out on the reef. The sound of the pounding surf could be heard across the island.

FEBRUARY

Most of my leisure time during daylight hours was still dedicated to improving my swimming and diving abilities and together with the lads from the billet, going out to explore the lagoon reef. However, leisure time after dark was becoming a bit of a bore. We had the NAAFI Club for a meal and the odd drink or three, or there was the Gan cinema, called the 'Astra'. They changed the films every couple of days, but these were not always to our taste. There was also the disadvantage that the cinema had a corrugated iron roof, so when it rained you could not hear the soundtrack no matter how much they turned the volume up.

Radio Gan

I cannot remember who first suggested the idea of having a Gan radio station, but I know everyone thought this would be a good idea. The NAAFI shop sold small transistor radio sets, so being able to tune in would not be a problem. What was needed however, was a suitable transmitter that could transmit on a frequency within the range of the available radios.

I seem to remember that a Sq/Ldr Murray, who was in charge of the Commcen, tasked me with having a first look around to see if anything was available or adaptable. He was fully aware that I had been working on Hithadhoo at the transmitter station with the civilian guys from Marconi. Sq/Ldr Murray, for his part, said that he would see if he could obtain some money to get the radio station going.

In the meantime I contacted Neil Drayfus of Marconi and was delighted to hear that he was just about to dispose of a 1 kilowatt transmitter over the reef. It radiated on 1.2 mhz in the medium waveband and so met our requirements exactly. This transmitter had been used for inter-island voice communication between Gan and Hithadhoo prior to more permanent channels being established.

Sq/Ldr Murray had been in contact with the Nuffield Organisation and they had come up trumps by promising an initial donation of £250 to buy equipment, then further donations per month for records and additional equipment once we became established.

The "Radio Gan Story" was about to begin.

It became such a large part of my, and many other people's, leisure time on Gan that elsewhere in these ramblings I have dedicated a whole chapter to it.

Work

I continued to work on Hithadhoo until the middle of February when the job I had been given was completed. I returned to Gan and worked as day staff at the CCS/Receiver station under W/O Marsh. He indicated that I would soon have to go on shift work.

Leisure

It was also in early February, whilst out on the reef off Gan, that I managed to rip off a large chunk of my ankle on the coral. Anti-coral ointment was obtained from the MO at the Gan Hospital in order to help the healing process but unfortunately he would not allow me to go swimming as the wound had to be kept dry. Coral cuts have to be treated if they are to heal properly. Something picked up from the coral inhibits the healing process and any wound will not scab over unless it is treated.

The Hospital

The RAF Hospital on Gan was very modern and had a fully equipped operating theatre. It was not only there to serve RAF personnel, but had special clinics set up and run for the Maldivian population in the Addoo Atoll. Quite a number of the local Maldivians suffered from Elephantiasis.

> 'This disease of the lymphatic system is characterised by an enormous enlargement of the infected area with the skin hardening and resembling the hide of an elephant. The disease is usually the result of a blockage of the lymphatic system by threadlike filarial worms, usually transmitted by mosquitoes. Most frequently affected parts of the body are the limbs and the genitals. The disease is normally treated by administration of an antifilarial drug and with surgery.'

Microsoft Encarta, 1996

It was very fortunate for one of the local Maldivians that the hospital was now fully established on Gan. The Maldivian in question was working for the AMWD and he was part of a working party on Hithadhoo strengthening and repairing the rather unstable jetty. He had the unfortunate experience of treading on a 'stone fish' whilst working in the water on the shallow reef.

These fish belong to the genus *Synanceja* and are found both in the Indian and Pacific oceans. They have a robust body which is about 14 inches long and this is covered with wartlike lumps and fleshy flaps. The fish has a large head and poisonous dorsal fins. They lie camouflaged and motionless amongst rocks or coral to await their prey. Since they are sand-coloured it makes them virtually impossible to see once they are stationary.

The Maldivian was barefoot, as were most of his colleagues and he was stung directly through the sole of his foot. The body's reaction to this is almost immediate. First comes intense pain and this is quickly followed by severe swelling of the limb affected.

Luckily the RAF Pinnace was at Hithadhoo and they got the Maldivian on board quickly. The hospital was contacted and the 45 minute journey back to Gan began. By the time the boat reached the jetty the Maldivian's leg had swollen to nearly three times its normal size and he was in agonising pain.

Once in hospital, the medical team immediately administered the necessary drugs and the patient, after a few days, made a full recovery. If the boat had not been at Hithadhoo, then the delay in getting this Maldivian to hospital for treatment would have almost certainly resulted in his death.

One RAF Airman also had reason to be grateful that there was a hospital on Gan. He and a friend had been standing outside the NAAFI Club, opposite billet 47 and the latter had been showing him his latest acquisition bought at the NAAFI shop. This was one of the latest underwater fishing spear guns powered by a number of strands of extremely thick bands of elastic.

What possessed his friend to load the spear gun we will never know, but the next scene we saw from our room in the billet was the airman on his back, on the ground, with a four-foot long spear sticking out of his chest. By their very nature, spear guns are designed to be fired under water and not in free air where they will obviously travel much further and faster. By the time we reached this unpleasant scene his colleague had already run into the NAAFI to phone for an ambulance.

He was rushed to hospital and immediately operated on in order to remove the spear. This was not an easy task as the spear tip had reverse-angled and barbed tines. We understood the operation went on for some three hours or more, during which time the airman lost a lot of blood.

The last we heard about him was that he was evacuated to a hospital in Singapore and eventually returned to the UK for further treatment. We were later told that he had suffered brain damage due to oxygen starvation during one of his operations. A very sad end to one airman's tour of Gan.

The result of this very unpleasant incident was that spear guns of any type were totally banned from use on or around Gan and the NAAFI shop withdraw all its stock from sale.

Billet Moving

When I first moved into billet 47, room 7, one of the airmen, whose bed was opposite to mine and who worked with me at the CCS/Receiver station was called Roger. I cannot remember exactly how many years he had signed on for in the RAF, but it was a considerable number. His full name was Roger Onward Hobart Honey, a name that is simply unforgettable. He did explain that the Hobart name came from a great, great grandfather who had spent all his life at sea, starting as a cabin boy and eventually becoming a captain. In similar vein, another of his past relations, had been a great explorer and had the name 'Onward' as a nickname.

It was nearing the end of February and we were told that Billet 47 was to be redecorated and that, as a temporary measure whilst the work was being done, everyone would have to be re-housed. Both ROH Honey and I were moved into spare beds in Billet 52, room 5. The four existing occupants, who all worked in HQ, seemed to resent the arrival of Roger and I from the Comms billet and certainly did nothing to make us feel welcome.

One of them especially, seemed to be totally bored with his tour of Gan. He never appeared to do anything apart from going to work. He certainly did not go swimming and I cannot ever recall seeing him in the NAAFI. He would spend many hours on his back in his pit, either sleeping or looking through a pair of binoculars he had purchased in the NAAFI shop at anything that decided to reside on the billet room ceiling. He would literally spend hours looking at chit-chats, flies, mosquitoes, spiders or any thing else on the ceiling and whilst engaged in this pursuit did not talk to anyone else. They really were a funny lot and we both looked forward to returning to our old billet.

Stand by your Beds

On February 25th, all airmen were issued with 'Dunlopillo' mattresses and all the existing ones were disposed of. We were told that the new mattresses were far more hygienic and would be better at resisting the infestations commonly found in the older types. They were certainly more comfortable than the old ones, but also felt hotter to sleep on, but we soon became used to them.

February came to an end, the coral wound on my ankle had now healed and I could go swimming and snorkelling on the reef again. I still had the odd trip to Hithadhoo to work and the pleasure of the company of the dolphins during the boat trip. My leisure time in the evenings was being taken up more and more with Radio Gan.

I had now been on Gan 71 days. Only 294 days left to go!

MARCH

On Gan in March the sun is directly overhead and at its hottest, however the following incident shows just how fickle the weather can be in the tropics. I have recorded below the exact words of a letter home that I sent on the 4th March 1960.

The 'Hastings' incident

It all started on Wednesday afternoon, 02-03-60, with some very heavy black clouds. It started to rain like the devil and then came the lightning. I have never seen anything quite like it before, really fantastic and quite frightening. Luckily the storm centre did not come directly over the island and the lightning at its nearest was about four miles away.

By 6 o'clock in the evening it was really dark except when lightening struck; then you could have easily taken a photograph. We all knew that a four-engined RAF Hastings was due in from Katunayake with 20 people on board and we wondered what sort of a journey they were having. There were twelve lads from Kat who were coming to Gan to catch a Britannia back to England, along with the CO of Kat who was also going home and the rest, who were the crew.

At about 6:30pm we heard the aircraft overhead and went out on the veranda of the billet to see it land. You could see it fairly clearly in the flashes of lightning. The aircraft came in on its first approach, landed on the wet runway but obviously misjudged its speed and touchdown point, and could not stop before reaching the end of the runway. The pilot was very aware of the situation and opened up all engines and managed to take off again. As you know the runway runs the entire length of the island and if an aircraft does overshoot, then it lands up in the sea. It is not very deep until reaching the reef edge but then can go down very quickly to a great depth.

However, back to the aircraft. After taking off again, the pilot apparently radioed the tower to say he was coming around for another approach. That was the last the tower heard from him. After waiting for a few minutes to make quite sure he wasn't coming in, the whole of the Gan crash service went into action.

One of the Search and Rescue Shackletons took off and very quickly located the Hastings in the sea about 3-4 miles from the end of the runway. The Shackleton crew directed the High Speed Launches to the scene and all the passengers and crew were picked up. When the launches reached the crash scene all the personnel were in rubber life rafts. Luckily no one was injured, just a few bruises here and there, the most unfortunate part being that everyone had lost all their personal kit as well as presents destined for those back home.

Apparently when the Hastings hit the sea, two of the engines detached, as did the wheels and undercarriage assemblies. This reduced the overall weight of the aircraft quite a bit and it remained afloat for some time, giving everyone time to get out. The Hastings eventually sank in about 100 fathoms (600 feet) of water. The wheels were still floating the next morning and were picked up by one of the launches.

As to the cause of the crash, nobody seems to know. The pilot said he thought he was landing on the runway and it seems he could have mistaken the Gan Channel shipping buoys as the runway markers. The cloud cover was down to 300 feet, the rain was pelting down and of course it was lightning every few seconds. Not exactly the conditions required for a landing at night. We understand that a court of enquiry is going to be set up."

Birthday Boy

My birthday arrived on Saturday March 5th and five of us decided to go to the pictures as the start of a celebration. The Astra was showing Frank Sinartra in *Hole in the Head* and Peter Sellers in *The Mouse that Roared*. It rained during the second film and you could not hear a thing due to the noise of the rain on the corrugated iron roof. The mandatory cartoon film was also shown with the end credits getting there customary greeting from the audience of "Good old Fred!" referring of course to the producer Fred Quimby of *Tom & Jerry* fame.

After the films we all went back to the NAAFI club to celebrate in the usual way until we were eventually thrown out.

Visitors

The Royal Navy Aircraft Carrier HMS *Centaur* arrived on March 8th and moored just off the Gan jetty in the lagoon. It had brought Aviation Spirit and Oil for the Gan storage tanks.

It always amazed us how the sea would boil with sharks every time the carrier kitchen staff dumped waste, which included meat, over the ship's side into the lagoon. This scene acted as quite a sobering thought when you were dinghy sailing in the lagoon in a strong wind or snorkelling well out from the reef edge. Most of us saw sharks at one time or another when out swimming, but I do not recall having heard of anyone being attacked or even threatened by them.

Mail

The Gan runway was fully operational again and aircraft were arriving on a regular basis. In spite of this the mail situation was really bad. So bad, that at least six of the lads wrote to their MPs, as well as complaining bitterly through the normal RAF channels. The CO became involved and promised to take some action.

New Arrivals

It was now March 21st and ten more 'moonies' arrived by Comet. When they walked into the mess they were greeted by the customary wolf whistles and jeering. Were we *really* like that when we arrived?

On Watch

Two of the CCS/Receiver station staff were allocated to a watch and I teamed up with Roger Onward Hobart Honey. Our watch times were:

07:00 to 12:30 hours & 18:15 to 24:00 hours

or 12:30 to 18:15 hours & 24:00 to 07:00 hours.

The daytime and evening watch shifts were fine and we managed to cope with those OK, but the shift between midnight and seven the next morning was an absolute killer. Neither Roger or I had worked on a 24-hour shift system before and our body clocks took a considerable time to readjust. At 03:00 hours everything was telling your body that it really should be asleep but you knew that a charge would be the likely result if you did drop off. I lost count of the number of cups of tea and coffee we consumed on our first night shift. I do recall going back to the billet after this first shift, dropping on the pit and sleeping very soundly for eight solid hours. Neither of us even bothered with breakfast.

Our ability to cope with these hostile times did get better and in the quieter moments of the watches we would write letters or play the odd game of chess. Very early in the morning, if we had little to do and everything was running OK, then I or Roger would go outside the building just before sunrise and climb some 20 to 30 feet up the passive reflector aerial mast so as to obtain a clear view of the sunrise over the eastern end of the runway and Indian Ocean horizon. This was always a magnificent sight, especially if there were a few clouds about and it never ceased to amaze me as to just how quickly the sun caused a noticeable rise in the air temperature. It was always a humbling, relaxing and pleasurable experience and certainly a great way to finish a night watch.

During morning and afternoon watches we always had a visit from the NAAFI wagon. On board were bottled cold drinks that could be purchased. 'Ganade' was a fizzy lemonade drink manufactured on Gan. Later in the year they added an orange drink to their range. Both were excellent thirst quenchers.

In HOT water

Relations with the HQ bodies in our new billet seemed to be thawing just a little and we did get the occasional "Good Morning", etc. By the end of the month we were all on Christian name terms.

The most significant event to occur at the end of March was that hot water became available in all the Airmen's Billets. As I said in a letter home at the time, and I quote: "You'll never believe it but I have just had my first hot bath in four months. The last was in Ceylon. I thought I was brown until today but am now six shades lighter. Dirty devil. They put the hot water on a couple of days ago, so I should be able to get my civvy shirts a little cleaner now, or should I say that Mohammed will be able to, on my behalf. It's amazing where all the dirt comes from and it really is a treat to have a hot shower once again."

APRIL

The weather in April started hot with a gentle breeze and just a few white puffy clouds. It was absolutely great. My leisure time during the day was spent snorkelling over the reef, sunbathing, or just sitting on the beach reading a book. In the evenings, when I was not on watch at the CCS building, I would either be in the Radio Gan studio or control room or just watching the sun go down.

Officers?

How is it that the Officers in the RAF always manage to perform even the simplest of tasks by using a different approach to that normally taken by NCOs and Airmen? I suppose that some may call this initiative or enterprise, whilst others may call it something else. Take, for instance, the simple task of fishing. First obtain a rod and suitable line, hook, and some bait, either dead or alive. Take your fishing tackle to an appropriate river bank or seashore, bait the hook, adjust the float level and cast into the water. What could be simpler? For comfort take a seat to rest on and wait for your first bite. That, I suggest, is how you and I would go about the simple task of fishing.

Not so for some of the officers on Gan. I sat on the beach one afternoon watching a certain Flight Lieutenant, who shall remain nameless, fishing in the deep water channel, just off the Officers' Mess, between Gan and Feydhoo.

There he was complete with rod, line and sinker, sitting on a small metal folding seat, whilst puffing away at a well-used pipe. The picture of absolute contentment.

I had snorkelled over this deep water channel a number of times and would guess that, at its deepest point, it was some 40 feet deep. There were always plenty of fish there, especially small groups of Barracuda as well as Parrot fish. It was therefore no surprise when the Flt/Lt's float disappeared and he started to reel in the line. I did not recognise the type of fish he had caught but it seemed to be some 20 inches in length and at a guess weighed in at some 10 to 15 lbs. Not bad at all for the first catch of the day.

It was after he had re-baited his hook and recast his line that I noticed something unusual. Where this intrepid fisherman's line entered the sea there appeared a great disturbance in the water. I thought to myself that he must have thrown in great quantities of ground bait and that it was all the fish attacking this that was the cause of all the commotion.

Not so, it was one of the Maldivian boys complete with swimming goggles. His presence in the water now became clear as he caught hold of the Flt/Lt's float and guided it carefully and slowly so that the hook, with bait attached, was just in front of an unsuspecting fish. The fish took a bite and "hey presto" up came another catch.

Now that's what I really call "cheating"!

It turned out that the young Maldivian was the Officer's room boy and for an extra modest payment would help in catching the fish in this way. Having been brought up on the islands, fishing and swimming were second nature to these boys. They would even target particular types and size of fish if requested to do so.

I now fully realised just why the fishing contest, scheduled for Christmas Day, had been called off. I suppose that's why we were the 'erks' and they were 'officers'!

Divine Spirit

Up until the beginning of April, wines and spirits could not be purchased in the Airmen's NAAFI, except at Christmas, or could be sold to airmen at the NAAFI shop. As from April 2 they *could* be purchased and a number of airmen began drinking to excess and were to be seen staggering about. This situation did not last very long and once the initial novelty wore off and bank balances were depleted, everyone started behaving responsibly again.

The Builders

Just to the rear of Billet 52, a new Airmen's billet was under construction. The workforce was about 30 strong and consisted of both Pakistanis and Maldivians. There was always a great deal of oriental discussion taking place and much gesticulating with the hands with everyone telling everyone else just what to do. I suppose this could have had something to do with the fact that the Maldivian workers did not understand the Pakistanis and vice versa. The billet did eventually get completed.

The Smell, etc.

The weather in early April had begun nice enough but by the end of the first week it had rained its hardest and vast areas of Gan, especially the areas around the Billets and Airmen's Mess, had become flooded. If you had to leave your billet then you had to wade through the residual water carrying your footwear with you. If you were on your way to the Mess then you had to use the tap thoughtfully provided just outside the entrance door to wash your legs and feet down before entering.

The floods gradually receded as the weather once again warmed up but the residue left behind was salt stained and very smelly. The smell slowly got better but the mosquitoes were having a field day and their population increased rapidly. In spite of the AMWD Hygiene department spraying the stagnant pools of water that still remained around the billets the mosquitoes were giving me hell again. My blood must have been different to everyone else's in the billet as I seemed to be the one most often targeted by the little sods. Our room's 'Flit' spray worked overtime, but even so, everyone was bitten at some time or another.

Work and Play

By the middle of April, I had been taken off the watch system and was once again working days, but this was for just a week. Roger had to go to Singapore to take an RAF education test and so it was back on watch for me, with another member of our team, until Roger returned. I spent the whole of Easter working on watch.

For all this work, as a National Service Airman with the rank of Junior Technician, I received the weekly wage of £2 and 11 shillings per week. I was therefore very pleased to be offered a *paid* part time job by the NAAFI, to repair radios broken in transit to the shop. I accepted this job with gratitude and started on the first of a great backlog of broken radios immediately. Most of these radios had only minor damage. The majority had cracked cases and/or the tuning mechanism had become broken or detached. Any money to help supplement my RAF wages was therefore gratefully received. It also helped in providing knock down priced radios for those airmen wishing to listen in to Radio Gan, my other great interest.

The RAF's interest in keeping us comfortable continued and to supplement the Dunlopillo mattresses previously issued we were now issued with bedspreads. We even had a choice of colours, blue, green or pink. I chose blue. There were certainly not many takers for the pink!

By the end of the month Roger had returned from Singapore after a successful education test. He had brought back for me the face mask that I had asked him to get, and someone else, who was leaving Gan, had given me their now redundant flippers. I was now all set for exploring the reef still further without having to borrow someone else's gear.

My leisure time was now fully committed and what with the announcing and controlling at Radio Gan, repairing the damaged NAAFI radios and getting as much time in as possible snorkelling the reef, life was pretty hectic, but also very enjoyable. I was now fully accustomed to life in the tropics and living an island existence. It was all good fun and a wonderful experience which no one could take away.

My work commitment for the RAF was also very enjoyable and it was good to be working on the equipment that my civilian employer, IAL, had designed and manufactured.

MAY

May, according to the meteorologists, is the official start of the monsoon season which then extends right through to November. Early May certainly lived up to its reputation and it rained solidly for a couple of days. This had the undesirable effect of bringing out the mosquitoes in hordes and, as usual, I was one of their favourite targets. It continued to rain on and off throughout the month although we did have some sunny days when of course the humidity rocketed.

All Change

Having just got used to our new friends in billet 52, room 5, Roger and I had to move back to billet 47, room 7, with some of the other lads who worked at the CCS/Receiver station. I was still working on shift and was put in charge of a watch. That meant our actions were not constantly monitored by a Sergeant. What freedom!

May was becoming a bit of a dull and uninteresting month, that is, until a new CO arrived. He really made himself unpopular by starting parade rehearsals for an AOC's inspection due on the 23rd May. I breathed a sigh of relief as I was going to be on watch on that date.

My relief however was short lived and I was told that I would have to go on at least one of the rehearsals just to make the numbers up. One hour, attempting to march up and down out on the pan in brilliant sunshine in the middle of the afternoon left everyone very, very hot to say the least. Our KD became three shades darker as it became ever wetter and shoes became attached and uncomfortable puddles of sweat.

It was very apparent that no one's heart was really in the parade rehearsals in such hostile conditions and everyone prayed to the local rain god for a well timed downpour. No such luck unfortunately and rehearsals continued each afternoon, usually just after lunch. Even the Officers were giving the impression that they were sorry for putting us Airmen through such an ordeal, but they had their orders from the CO and that was that. Everyone wished Wing Commander Thomas was back in charge as he would not have even contemplated such a parade.

Relaxation

The best thing to do when the weather on Gan was so humid was to go into the sea swimming and snorkelling and this I did at every opportunity. I was accompanied on most of my trips by SAC Jack Findlay who was an aerial rigger and who had recently agreed to be my controller at Radio Gan after a certain amount of arm twisting on my part.

Jack was a Scotsman from Prestonpans in East Lothian, Scotland, who liked his drink, whisky in particular, and was an excellent swimming teacher. His Scots accent was so broad that, at first, I and everyone else found him hard to understand. It was Jack's accent that initially put him off the idea of joining Radio Gan as he thought that he would have to do some announcing. I assured him that he would not have to do this and he took to the task of controlling like a veteran.

As far as I was concerned he continued the good work that Harry had started in improving my swimming and diving capabilities. By the end of the month I could swim, without flippers or mask, at least 120 yards with no problem at all.

A Bit of a Break

Just a few days before the AOC's inspection, when everyone was supposedly cleaning and dusting everything and floors were being given that extra shine, a Maldivian, working down a hole near to the Airmen's Mess, caused chaos by putting his pickaxe through the signals cable between the CCS/Receiver building and the Communications Centre. Luckily such an eventuality had been foreseen and a spare cable via an alternative route had been laid. This was put into service and signals traffic re-established fairly quickly. It was fully operational again after about 4 hours.

AOC's Inspection

The 23rd arrived and the AOC's parade on the pan started at 0700 hrs. Unfortunately, from most people's point of view, it did not rain, but having the parade at that time in the morning meant that temperatures were slightly more tolerable for those unfortunate airmen who had been 'lumbered'.

Roger and I were on watch until midnight the previous evening and were scheduled for the 1200 hr to 1800 hr watch on inspection day. The CO and AOC were visiting all sections of the camp and duly arrived at the CCS/Receiver building at around 1530 hrs. I was introduced to the AOC by WO Marsh and asked if I could give the AOC a tour of the building and explain exactly what we did and how we did it.

I thought this task may be a little intimidating, but in spite of all the 'scrambled egg', the AOC was an extremely pleasant and knowledgeable man and what was a little frightening, knew just why I had been posted to Gan to work in the Communications Control Section. He was also very aware of the complexities of all the new equipment and asked many very pertinent questions about its operation.

He left with the CO and the rest of the entourage after about an hour, seeming well pleased with his visit. Everyone then breathed an enormous sigh of relief, including me.

To give our CO credit he did issue a notice to everyone the day following the inspection thanking everyone for their efforts and saying how pleased and impressed the AOC had been with his tour of all the sections of the camp.

The CO then crowned this with the suggestion that he was thinking of introducing swimming restrictions. According to the CO, whose first overseas posting was Gan, the reef was extremely dangerous and he was suggesting that before anyone could go swimming then they must be able to do 50 yds breast stroke, 50 yds crawl and 50 yds freestyle.

Just how he was going to implement such a stupid ruling we did not know. In the first place who was actually going to test the 400 RAF residents on Gan? Was he going to test each visiting Navy rating or transiting passenger who visited the island before allowing them to go into the sea? Everyone knew it was not a practical proposition and like most of the new rules this out-of-touch CO tried to introduce, it fell by the wayside.

Out of Bounds

The end of May was nearly with us and the weather was even hotter than normal. In spite of Feydhoo being 'out of bounds' to all RAF personnel, Jack, Terry and I were invited by Mohammed, yet another, the number three man on Feydhoo, to visit his home. Mohammed used to work during the day keeping our CCS/Receiver building spotlessly clean and even though we could not speak each other's language we managed to get by with a mix of hand signs and drawing of pictures. We gratefully accepted his kind offer and agreed to visit his home the following Sunday.

The day arrived and we hired a *dhoni* from one of the locals and rowed across the short stretch of sea to Feydhoo, trying our hardest to look like locals on a fishing expedition. We thought it was well worth taking the chance of getting caught by the RAF police just to see how the Maldivians really lived and to get off Gan for a couple of hours.

Mohammed was waiting on the beach for us and took us through the palms to his house just a short distance away from the beach. He lived with his wife, children and members of his family in one of the prefabricated houses supplied by the RAF as part of an agreement between the British and Maldivian governments for the re-housing of locals displaced by the RAF from Gan.

His house, like all the other houses we saw on Feydhoo, was spotlessly clean and tidy. His wife was making a necklace from silver thread on a linen covered ball, about 8 inches in diameter, fixed to a stand on the table. The silver thread was wound on bobbins similar to those used for lace making in the UK. The necklace being produced looked very intricate and very pretty.

The beds for the babies and younger children were of the hammock type and were slung from fixings in the roof, whilst their parents slept in conventional beds.

Feydhoo 1960. Typical prefabricated houses as supplied by the MOD and erected by the AMWD.

Feydhoo 1960. Typical Maldivian hand built houses.

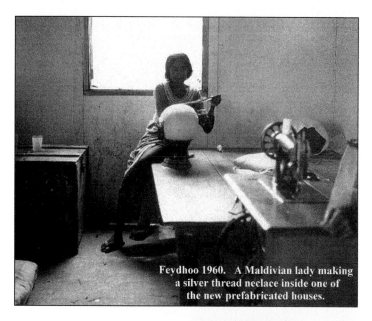

Feydhoo 1960. A Maldivian lady making a silver thread neclace inside one of the new prefabricated houses.

Feydhoo 1960. Maldivian men bringing home local produce.

Feydhoo 1960. Maldivian brother and sister outside their home.

We all felt very privileged to have been allowed into Mohammed's house and thanked him and his wife very much. We then, with his blessing, continued to explore the rest of the island.

The traditionally built houses we saw were made almost entirely of woven palm branches and had earth floors. Most houses appeared to have chickens around them and one or two we saw obviously kept other livestock.

The native Maldivian women washed their hair and then soaked it in an oil extracted from the coconut which was then perfumed. This gave their long black hair a wonderful sheen.

We continued our walk around the island and Jack met a Maldivian lad who used to be his room boy. He spoke very good English and acted as our guide for the rest of our visit. All the locals were very friendly and would readily accept a cigarette when offered.

The children were very excited to see us on their island and wanted us to have a game of football with them. They all looked very well cared for with most having very round and fat stomachs through eating too much rice.

All the children up to about six years old ran around with nothing on and the older ones just wanted their pictures taken with us. One youngster aged about six, a boy, tagged on to us and followed us around the island wherever we went. Jack offered him a cigarette which he took and put in his pocket. Either this was for a crafty smoke later or he was going to give it to his dad or elder brother. Jack's ex-room boy would not tell us, so we assumed it was the former.

We were soon joined by yet another boy who was about 4 years old who informed us via his friend that he wanted a cigarette as well. Jack gave him one and he immediately put it in his mouth and asked for a light. He could not have been more than three feet tall. We all stood by waiting for him to turn green, or whatever colour native boys turn, and to start coughing. To our amazement nothing happened and he puffed away like a 20-a-day man.

Most of the small girls on the island were very shy and would quickly hide when they saw us walking in their direction. The women and older girls were not quite so reticent and did wave to us and pose with their babies for us to photograph.

We had all enjoyed a great day and it was a wonderful experience. The men were coming home from their work on the island and the "Duty Bat Squadron" were gathering in the palms for their return trip to Gan, so we said our goodbyes and through Jack's ex-room boy thanked everyone for making us so welcome. We returned to the *dhoni* and rowed back to Gan in time for the evening meal quickly followed by a welcome drop of beer in the NAAFI. A really great day and we didn't get caught either, which made it even better.

JUNE

We had been given six days leave over the Whitsun period and every day it had been sunshine all the way. What little rain there had been had fallen at night. Jack's tour on Gan was rapidly coming to an end and he was due to fly out around the 12th July. He only had about 48 days to do so was becoming in a more buoyant mood as every day passed and his "chuff factor" approached infinity.

Jack, Harry, a number of the lads from the billet and I all went swimming over the reef every day over Whitsun and had a really great time. It was on one of these trips that I nearly managed to drown myself whilst attempting to see just how far down I could dive wearing my snorkel mask. I had perhaps managed to get down some twenty feet when the pressure of the water overcame the sealing properties of the air valve. This resulted in water rushing into the face mask and in my panic me trying to take a breath. The result was yours truly surfacing at a rapid rate of knots and trying to replace sea water with air after wrenching off the mask and coughing my heart out. Everyone else thought it was very amusing! I didn't, but had learnt my lesson and did not attempt to go so deep again, besides the water felt pretty cold at that depth. Ten feet down was quite far enough.

After Whitsun, the weather turned really nasty again and we had many hours of solid rain. Billets were becoming islands yet again and trying to find an un-flooded route to the Airmen's Mess was now impossible, you just had to wade through the stagnant pools of water and carry your footwear. I braced myself for the inevitable increase in the mosquito population.

Roger and I were on watch again and on nights. Luckily we always had a lift in a Jeep or covered lorry to the CCS/Receiver site so at least we managed to keep dry.

The Queen's Birthday

One thing you soon learn after joining the RAF is to keep your head down, never volunteer for anything and only speak if spoken to. I thought that I had managed this quite well up to now. I was reminded of an incident in basic training at RAF Bridgnorth, when Sergeant Prescott in charge of our flight (7th) enquired if anyone was interested in bike racing. As he expected, and hoped, about five arms were raised and he picked on one airman and told him to come out to the front. He then proceeded to tell him, in front of everyone else, that his bike was parked just round the corner and had a puncture. He told him there was a repair kit in the bag on the bike and he had 20 minutes to fix it. I think we all felt quite sorry for the airman, but it did teach everyone not to volunteer, however indirectly, for anything.

My guided tour of the CCS/Receiver building for the AOC had obviously not gone by unnoticed by the CO and I received an invitation from the Government Representative in the Maldives to attend a celebration in the Officers Mess of the Queen's Birthday. Looking back I suppose it must have been a great honour to be asked to attend as the Communications Section representative, but I did not quite see it like that at the time.

Some of the suggestions from my fellow workers and room mates as to why I had been asked were extremely rude and I countered their suggestions by saying that I was the only one who had a decent pair of trousers, white shirt *and* RAF tie to go as their representative.

This didn't seem to make much difference to their attitude and I was asked if I would like to borrow some additional underpants. I couldn't think why!

I turned up at the Officers' Mess slightly apprehensive and was met by the Government representative. He immediately put me at ease and we had a long discussion on the merits of National Service. I have great respect for these guys and it is very easy to see just why they are diplomats. Being nice and being able to talk to anyone, every day, irrespective of their race, creed, colour or political persuasion must be very difficult.

I was eventually introduced to the CO and when he had determined just where I worked and what I did, he said, "I do like drains, do you"? Now, not being a drain man myself, I found I was a little short on words at this point and fell back to talking about the recent heavy rains we had experienced. This was apparently why the question on drains had come up as they had to fit a new drain just outside the CO's office to stop station HQ from flooding. I suppose the Officers knew this fact but I certainly did not.

His question to me just confirmed what I and everyone else had thought about him for some time and I spent the rest of a very pleasant evening avoiding another meeting with this 'funny' man.

Rule Number XXX

By the 20th of the month the CO had further alienated himself from most of the RAF personnel on Gan by banning all nude bathing and sunbathing on the island. According to him this practice offended the Pakistanis who worked for AMWD. We made our own enquiries via our Pakistani friends and they told us that they knew of no one complaining. It was pretty obvious to us that the CO was once again allowing his own prejudices to dictate the rules he thought should apply to everyone else. We all thought that if he carried on like this then very shortly he would have a mutiny on his hands.

Nearly everyone, Officers and Airmen, visited the long strip of beach just north of the eastern runway end at some time or another and sunbathed minus their swimming trunks. The beach was not near to any occupied buildings or roads and was just about as far as possible from the Pakistani camp as it was possible to get. It was therefore ideal for skinny dipping. I suppose it must have something to do with man's primeval instinct of trying to return to nature. Swimming starkers just has to be experienced at least once in your life.

We were always very discreet when we heard a plane about to take off, or approaching the runway to land, by either going into the sea or turning face down in the sand. We certainly had no intention to shock any passengers, female or male, who happened to be looking out of the planes' windows.

When the Navy were in port then they never worried about such niceties and would swim naked on the usual beach just by the Officers' Mess whether or not ladies who were stopping over for a few hours were in the sea or on the beach.

Great News

On the 25th June the CO unexpectedly left the island for a new unspecified posting. Now that was a surprise, I don't think. It just showed what a well orchestrated underground movement could achieve when really pushed. It had been obvious for some time that even the Officers had become totally disenchanted with the CO's totally irrational rules and regulations. His replacement had much more liberal ideas, he had served overseas many times before and knew exactly what to do to keep up the morale of all the men on his station. Our special beach at the end of the island was once again open for its original use and the new CO joined us there on a number of occasions. Peace had once again returned to our island paradise.

Moving Again?

Yet once again this month, Roger and I and the rest of the lads in our room had to move billet. This time it was to billet 54, the new billet, and to room 7. It really was very smart and much better than the old one. Our room was two tone with a white ceiling and ceiling fan, green floor, walls dark green at the bottom and light green at the top. Each bed had an individual bed light. Even the beds and lockers were new and best of all there were no holes in the 'mozzy nets' covering the windows and doors.

Phew!

The month ended with the weather turning very hot again with temperatures well above 100F in the shade. Even Jack was complaining that it was too hot although he only had about 15 days left to do. He was scheduled to leave on a Britannia on the 12th July.

I had now completed six months on Gan and was looking forward to my holiday break in Singapore.

JULY

Early July started with very strong winds which died down for a few days and then returned with a vengeance around the 10th. The weather then deteriorated badly and it rained all through the day with strong winds which blew down many palm branches. The Pinnace could not put out to Hithadhoo until very late in the afternoon to deliver food and mail to the guys at the transmitter station. The boat crew had a very uncomfortable ride getting there. We were told that the weather was coming from the tail end of a typhoon that had hit India a few days earlier.

I woke up on the morning of the 11th to find my bed virtually surrounded by water which had blown under the billet door during the night. What a mess. Luckily I had not left anything on the floor and with Mohammed's help we soon had the room looking ship shape again.

Go-Karting?

We were informed that a Gan Go-Karting Club was to be formed and that three karts were on the island already. This greatly appealed to me as I had always had a very keen interest in any form of motor racing and had taken part in and organised a number of car rallies before coming into the RAF. The idea was to run heats each week, on the aircraft pan, between the various camp sections and eventually to have a final between the top two teams. It was unfortunate, but during my time on Gan, this idea never came to fruition. There were apparently major problems over insurance cover for the drivers and the whole idea was temporarily suspended.

I understand that later in the life of Gan that the insurance problems were resolved and that a very active and professional Go-Karting club was set up.

UK at Last

Jack Findlay eventually left Gan on a Britannia on Monday 11th June one day earlier than scheduled. After some well deserved leave spent with his parents, sisters and their families, he was posted to RAF Henlow where he would finish his time in the RAF at the end of October. I have never seen anyone look so happy as he ascended the steps into the aircraft for his flight home. His first week at Henlow was not a happy one however as he got pulled up for having dirty webbing on the first parade he attended and was put on a charge.

Dirty Habits

Although I had smoked cigarettes on the odd occasion in the UK before joining the RAF, their high cost had put me off becoming a habitual user. However here on Gan cigarettes sold in the NAAFI cost one shilling for twenty and I had started smoking once again. Whisky was 1/6d for a double and beer was a 1/- a can. I soon realised that all the spirits and smoking were having a serious effect on my health. It was especially noticeable that I was short of breath when I went in swimming or snorkelling. I decided to once again quit smoking and just stick to drinking beer. I no longer had the influence of the whisky drinking Scotsman to lead me astray.

Hey Ho and Up She Rises

Mains power for the Hithadhoo transmitter station and all associated buildings normally came from the power station on Gan via an undersea cable. The Hithadhoo complex having its own back-up generator. This was just as well, as an incident occurred in July when a supplies boat dropped anchor just off Hithadhoo and when making ready to leave managed to pull up the mains cable with the anchor. The local power supply was immediately put into service and had to be used for a number of days until it could be confirmed by specialist divers that no damage had been done to the underwater supply cable.

Pedal Power

July 14th was the day when bicycles were issued to all airmen and NCOs. This was OK, but caused a certain amount of perspiration to be generated when cycling to work, especially during the day. It also led to the "Round Gan" Challenge race. All contestants had to completely circumnavigate Gan, using the roads, in the shortest possible time. Scrutineers were strategically placed to ensure that no cheating went on, but of course it did. I seem to recall the record was somewhere around 15 minutes and 10 seconds and was held by someone from the Fire Section. The best time for a challenge was just before sunset as this usually meant slightly lower temperatures and the advantage of being able to collapse at the NAAFI bar afterwards so as to replenish lost fluids.

Singapore Girl?

There was one distinct drawback to being marooned on Gan for a one year tour and that was the total lack of female company. This was particularly hard on those airmen who were married as it was an unaccompanied posting. The majority of us who were single had girl friends back in the UK and this caused quite a few problems as well.

Everyone had their own ways of coping with this situation. The solution for a large number of the guys was to find out when a transiting aircraft was due in and ascertain just how many of the passengers were female. At the appropriate time they would then stand outside the transit mess and wait for the bus to shed its load of passengers. All bulging eyes would then be on the female form that emerged. Catching a glimpse of a woman when we could, was about the best most of us could hope for.

If the transiting aircraft went unserviceable at Gan, and they often did, then this was a bonus as far as the airmen were concerned. If female passengers had time on their hands then what better way to spend it than by having a dip in the sea. When this happened you could hardly see the beach by the Officers' Mess for all the bodies on it. It may have cooled the lady passengers down but it had the reverse effect on the lads. I am quite sure that those lady passengers who wore Bikini swim suits had no idea just what effect they were having on us airmen.

Other airmen plastered the inside of their locker doors with cuttings taken from girlie magazines or from books obtained from under the counter shops in red light areas in the UK or Singapore. Some of these were so hot that it was surprising that the varnish on the outside of the locker doors had not blistered.

Most of us tried to keep in touch with those back home by writing letters at every opportunity. This was why the regular delivery of mail to the island was so important to everybody.

Everyone had the opportunity, after serving on Gan for 6 months, to take leave in Singapore. The flight was free but you paid for your own accommodation and food when you arrived.

Before you left for your holiday it was mandatory that you went to see the MO. He did not mix his words and left you in no doubt about the consequences of procuring a Singapore "Lady". The suggestion was that if you did, then you may come back with one more present than you had bargained for. He also reminded us National Servicemen of the film that was shown to all of us in the second week of basic training on Sexually Transmitted Diseases. I recall that some of the airmen who watched this film had to go out of the room before it ended as what they saw made them feel really sick. It was certainly very graphic and in full colour.

Leave

It was now the 15th July and my leave in Singapore was imminent. All that was required was a free seat on an aircraft.

A Comet arrived the following day and Harry from station HQ, Trevor the cook and I, all got a seat. Flying time to Singapore was 5 hours. We arrived in the evening of the 17th and went to stay at the "Sandes Soldiers Home" in Portsdown road.

Settling in

This home was open to all forces personnel, but it seemed that only RAF guys were in residence at that time. The charge for staying at this very pleasant place, including all meals, was $4.50 (Singapore) a day. This was the equivalent cost of about 10 shillings and 6 pence in old money. The home had many recreational facilities including a very large swimming pool complete with diving boards. It also had snooker tables, dart boards, a table tennis table, putting green, tennis courts, a library and a quiet room.

The whole place was run on the basis of Christian principles. Religion was not forced upon you but you were expected to behave in a decent and civilised way. Certainly swearing or returning late in a drunken stupor would be very much frowned upon and you would probably be asked to move somewhere else.

The bedrooms, with four beds in each, were well furnished and decorated even if the beds were a little on the hard side. We had obviously all been spoilt by the Dunlopillo mattresses on Gan. The Sandes Home warden would call on each bedroom in the morning to ensure that you had slept in your bed and not in someone else's in Singapore town.

Food was also great and you were very welcome to have as many helpings as you liked. The one thing I remembered most was the fact that you could obtain a glass of *fresh* milk. Only the powdered sort was available on Gan which was not pleasant at all.

When we arrived we were greeted by Colin and Tony the firemen who had flown out from Gan two days earlier than us. They suggested that they already knew some good, or was it bad, places to visit in town for a drink and some entertainment. We initially declined their kind offer and said we may join them later in the week.

We all soon dropped into a pretty lazy routine at the Sandes Home. We would get up at about 0900 hrs, then go to breakfast. Laze around the pool sunbathing for a couple of hours and then if we were feeling really energetic go for a swim.

Harry decided to see if all his efforts at getting me to swim properly during our early days on Gan had paid off, so he set me the challenge of completing, without stopping, 100 lengths of the 25 yard long pool. This was a challenge I just had to accept, especially as there was a wager on it and the possibility of some free beer at the end. I may not have been the worlds' quickest, but at least I stayed the course and at the end gave my swimming teacher the customary signal of victory.

I still remembered my early attempts in the water with Harry shouting encouraging words like, "Get your bloody head under", and "Keep your arse down". Then later, the attempts of Jack Findlay, in trying to increase my distance swimming when I was completely knackered by previous efforts, or was it the previous night's beer consumption?

It had all been worth the effort in the end and I have since spent many happy hours swimming and snorkelling at various tropical locations throughout the world. After our usual mornings sunbathing and swimming session at the Sandes Home it was time for lunch so we went and fed our faces yet once again. Most afternoons we caught the number "24" bus into Singapore town to see the sights and have the odd drink or two. Nothing too strenuous.

Singapore

First impression of Singapore was that this place was really in a mess. Nearly everywhere was filthy, dirty and smelt a great deal, especially around the moored Sampans and the river area.

The local people also made it very clear that you were none too welcome in the centre of town and it was certainly no place to be when it was dark.

Singapore was captured and occupied by the Japanese in 1942 and only liberated by British troops in September 1945.

Although it was now nearly 13 years since liberation there were many reminders that Singaporians did not give up their freedom easily. War damaged buildings still stood and many steel lamp posts were riddled with bullet holes. In 1959 Singapore had become a self governing state in the Commonwealth of Nations but due to the infiltration of communist activists from Malaya there was much political unrest in the territory. It was probably this unrest and uncertainty as to what the future held for them as a self governing state, that we faced a hostile reception from the populous in general. All visitors were treated with grave suspicion.

In spite of this, Harry, Trevor and I all visited a number of bars just for a drink or two. As soon as the bar girls knew we had come from Gan they were all over us and we had no option but to buy them drinks. They were soon sitting on our knees and trying to get us to go with them. "You come with me for nice time Mister?" or "Why don't you come and meet my Sister, she's *very* pretty?." Some of the girls were very attractive and certainly knew how to wind a guy up. I don't *remember* any of us cracking under the pressure and we left a number of disappointed ladies finishing their drinks on more than one occasion. *That* film we had seen in basic training came to mind on a number of occasions during our holiday. Which was exactly what it was meant to do I suppose.

We visited the Britannia Club on a number of occasions, as it was here that the number 24 bus stopped. The club was nearly always busy with personnel from each of the three services. At least here you could obtain a drink without being molested by bar girls. "Anchor" and "Tiger" bottled beer were the recommended brews served at the club. It was all very pleasant sitting in an air conditioned building with views looking out over the busy Singapore harbour. For the more energetic types there was also an outside swimming pool.

Shopping

We decided to do the majority of our shopping at Changi village near to the RAF airfield. The local shopkeepers here welcomed you with open arms and would do anything to keep you in their shop until all your requirements for purchasing items had been met. Bartering with them for the best price was expected and meant a lengthy stay if you really wanted to negotiate a good price. You were plied with ice cold drinks continuously whilst you bartered. When they insisted that this definitely was their lowest price, then you threatened to leave their shop. This almost always had the desired effect and a few more dollars were knocked off.

What was on show for sale in any particular shop bore little resemblance to the items that they would sell to you. You said what you wanted and one of the shop assistants would disappear to an adjoining shop that sold the item and then bring it back for your inspection and possible purchase. I do not know if the shop assistant bartered with his colleague before or after the eventual sale to you but everyone seemed happy to work this way and after all, each shop owner was obviously making a profit out of the sale, and that is what really mattered to them.

Singapore 1960. Sandes Soldiers Home, Portsdown Road.

Singapore 1960. Sandes Soldiers Home swimming pool.

Tiger Balm Gardens

Before leaving Singapore we were told that we really should visit the Tiger Balm Gardens.

These are not gardens in the conventional sense but contained stone and plaster effigies and models depicting many of the beliefs and superstitions of the Buddhist religion. Each model, or group of models represented one of these beliefs and we were fortunate in having an English speaking guide to explain just what each tabloid represented. We had had to barter with the guide prior to our tour as to how much he was going to charge us for his services. In course of conversation we found out he was a student at one of the colleges in Singapore and he needed the money to help pay for his accommodation and food. We felt quite sorry for him in that he had to resort to such means to support his schooling.

The Flicks

The day before returning to Gan we all decided that we wanted to see what a real cinema was like, so we booked tickets to go and see William Wyler's "Ben Hur" at the Lido Theatre in the centre of town. We went mad and paid 5$ Singapore for the seats which were in the circle. The film commenced at 2000 hrs on Sunday evening and we had seats 17 to 20 in row "F". What with the extra wide screen and excellent sound system at the Lido, the Astra on Gan was never going to be quite the same again. The Lido didn't have a tin roof either.

The film show finished about 2300 hrs and we caught the bus outside the Britannia club and returned to the Sandes Home and packed ready for our trip back to Gan.

Back to Gan

We departed RAF Changi, on Monday 25th July by way of an RAF Transport Command Comet. The journey back to Gan took just over 4 hours travelling at an average speed of 545 mph. I was not too sorry to leave Singapore because of the squalor that we had found. However, we were all glad of the break, the change of scenery and the rest and relaxation afforded by our stay at the Sandes Soldiers Home.

We arrived back from our leave in Singapore to find that there had been a major outbreak of Dysentery. Over half the airmen on the island had gone down with this far from pleasant disease. The Gan hospital beds were totally full and a complete barrack block had to be taken over to accommodate those who were sick. Every single person on the island had to take a number of pills to ensure that the spread of the disease could be halted. An officer from the medical staff personally supervised the daily taking of each pill dispensed to each person over the period of a week. The number of new cases quickly abated and luckily I was fortunate and did not catch the dreaded disease. It was thought that contaminated food served in the Airmen's Mess was the initial reason for the outbreak.

AUGUST

Bank holiday Monday came and it poured with rain all through the day. I wasn't very happy either as I was suffering from a boil in my right ear. It was extremely painful and apart from keeping me awake at night I was not allowed to go swimming. The MO prescribed some appropriate pills and potions and, knowing that I had recently returned from Singapore, asked if I wished to see him about anything else? I think his response to my reply was something on the lines of "oh, what a good boy!" He also said that he thought the boil was caused by a infection picked up in the swimming pool in Singapore.

HM Customs

Whilst we had been away a report had come through that Alex Cameron of AT&E, whom I had worked with earlier on the VF channelling equipment at Gan, had been arrested on his return to the UK from Singapore, by HM Customs. He had apparently tried to smuggle, in his firm's name, a considerable quantity of cheap watches and other items he had purchased in Singapore. His company were heavily fined, he was heavily fined and he also lost his job as a result. He was apparently very lucky to escape a term in jail.

All Change

By the second week in August, after a week of very hot weather, my ear had recovered sufficiently to allow me to go swimming again. The waterproof watch I had purchased in Changi village was performing well even if it did cost just £3 and 7 shillings.

At long last I came off the watch system and went back to working days. We worked 0700 to 1300 hrs Monday to Saturday inclusive. This meant that every afternoon, weather permitting, swimming was on the cards.

The original and picturesque BFPO 180 Post Office was moved to a new concrete based building opposite the HQ building and would not be used after Saturday 13th. It would then be demolished.

It rained solidly from the 16th to the 21st of the month when eventually the sun came out again. This was just as well as we were on the move again. Back to Billet 47 again, but this time to room 8 and not 7. Redecoration was now totally complete and wall lights and a two tone colour scheme were the order of the day. The weather remained very hot until the end of the month accompanied by the usual hordes of mosquitoes.

SEPTEMBER

August had been a pretty uneventful month so someone decided to test the resolve of our new Post Office by giving the parcels section a little extra work. In September it was all the rage to send complete coconuts back to the UK by post. The outside shell had to be painted black and the address then written on it with either yellow or white paint. The appropriate stamps were then stuck on. This apparently

RAF Gan. 1960. Airmen's Billet under construction

RAF Gan 1960. The Beach by the Officers Mess.

caused great mirth amongst the UK Postmen that had to deliver them. It didn't amuse our PO guys very much at all. The practice was self defeating in the end as the islands' supplies of black and yellow paint were depleted.

Our life of luxury continued with the issuing of Dunlopillo pillows to all airmen, to complement the mattresses and bed spreads already issued. What with having our own room boys to do the washing and ironing and to keep the place tidy we were really beginning to get used to this way of life. We did suggest to our Sergeant that to make life really complete that he should volunteer to bring us a cup of tea each morning before we got up. I leave his reply to your imagination. Basically it meant "NO".

Another fairly quiet month was nearly over and what with swimming each day in the hot sunshine my hair had been bleached white. I was probably now fitter than I had ever been in all my life due to the minimised calorie intake and the daily swimming exercise.

OCTOBER

We were soon jolted out of our soporific mood at the beginning of October by the arrival of four Valiant bombers and two Javelin fighters. The aircraft were scheduled to arrive around midday and we all took up strategic positions to get a good view of the landings. The Valiant aircraft are really large and weigh in at 34 tons when empty and up to 63 tons fully loaded.

The first three Valiants and the Javelins came in OK but the fourth Valiant burst tyres on landing and was left stranded and slued across the runway.

No one was hurt in the incident but the runway was blocked for about 1½ hours whilst they jacked the aircraft up and put on new wheel assemblies. There was little left of the original tyres.

Normally it wouldn't have mattered that the runway was blocked, but a Britannia was waiting to land so it had to fly around the Atoll for 1½ hours. We had never seen so many aircraft here all at once. 4 Valiants, 2 Javelins, 2 Shackletons, a Varsity and two Britannias. We were all sure the island would sink.

The Valiants and Javelins left Gan at about 2100 hrs. We were in Billet 47 which was situated no more than 400 yards from the end of the runway. The two Javelins took off together which generated quite a significant amount of noise but nothing compared to the Valiants which took off directly one after another. I really thought our billet was going to collapse with all the vibration caused by the departing aircraft. Each aircraft was taken to full throttle before the brakes were released for the take-off. You certainly had to cover your ears or it would have been just too painful.

No incidents this time and they all departed safely. It was however very noticeable the next day that a significant amount of the coral sand at the end of the runway had been blown away by these giants of the air during their departure phase.

New Arrivals

On the 3rd of the month a WVS worker arrived on the island. I quote directly from one of my letters home:-

"We now have a woman stationed here on Gan. She is a WVS worker called Miss Caton, who has come to organise and run the "Island Club". This will be a place where us airmen can go and get a reasonably priced meal and relax in rather more luxurious conditions than we can at the moment. I am sure she will make a very good job of it. She looks about 40 to 50 years old and looks the *very capable* sort. She keeps all the boys amused by waving at them (sorry us) when she sees us. It's quite a novelty to see one of the opposite sex. Quite a nice change."

Not only did we now have a resident lady on the island but the Navy were in port. This usually livened the place up and this time was no exception. Loads of nude navies bathing during the day and at night, very rude songs coming from the NAAFI club.

To give Miss Caton her due, she often used to join the residents of the NAAFI club in the evenings especially on a Saturday. As the evening wore on the songs would inevitably get more ribald and would then deteriorate into the downright filthy category. She would always take the hint when the songs were getting to this stage. Remarks from the lads like "I think it's past your bedtime June", or even more really subtle ones like, "Goodnight Miss Caton", would be uttered. She always took the hint and would leave gracefully before a full rendition of "Oh Sir Jasper", or "Mike Maginty's Ball" took place.

Hithadhoo Excursion

During the course of my daily work at the CCS/Receiver station I had to have regular telephone liaison with the lads that ran the transmitter station on Hithadhoo. One of these guys was Colin Orme and he and I arranged to meet on his day off on Hithadhoo with a view to exploring the island together. Like Feydhoo, most areas of the island were "out of bounds" to RAF personnel so we had to be discreet and selective as to just where we went.

Wednesday 5th was Colin's day off and I managed to hitch a ride over to Hithadhoo on the early morning Pinnace and met him at the shore end of the jetty. The day had started wet, but by 0830 hrs it had begun to clear up and the sun was out.

We decided to walk north, up the lagoon side road. The majority of the island is thickly wooded and there is some shade available to keep the worst of the sun of your back. The palms, however, did stop the sea breezes that we were used to on Gan from reaching you and the ambient temperature felt much higher.

The Boatyard

After walking for about a mile we came upon a boatyard where the local craftsmen were building Dhonis. All the frame members for the boats and the planks for the hull were hewn from solid wood and shaped by hand. We were amazed at the speed that these boat builders could work using just hand tools which were also made on the island. I believe the wood they used had to be shipped in from Ceylon.

The joints between each of the planks of the boat were made waterproof by the insertion of fine rope strands made from coconut fibres which were then coated with a type of locally made brown glue. No nails or screws were used in the construction of the boats and all the various joints were fixed by using wooden dowels.

The only metal we saw used on the boat was for the manufacture of the simple hinges used to connect the rudder to the transom. Originally this attachment would have been made using rope manufactured from the fibres of coconuts.

The "Buggalow"

We were also shown, in one of the locally constructed boat houses, a "Buggalow". This is an extremely large hand made boat complete with a cabin and designed for long ocean voyages. This particular boat was the one used by Mr Affa Didi, the Maldivian prime minister, when he visited Ceylon some two years earlier. The boat was only used on very special ceremonial occasions.

In size terms the Buggalow compared favourably with the RAF's Pinnace but did not have the luxury of an engine. The mast for the Buggalow must have been some 40 foot long and was housed in its own covered area alongside the main boatshed.

We both felt very privileged to have seen this ceremonial boat and thanked the boat builders for showing us such an historic craft.

The Lake

From the boatyard we made our way inland and eventually, after struggling through the thick vegetation, reached a large freshwater lake. We contemplated having a swim to cool off but as we did not know how deep the lake was or what lurked in its waters we decided against a dip. There were certainly plenty of mosquitoes about which kept us fully occupied.

We continued west across the island and eventually came out of the palms onto the beach. Here there was a gentle breeze, which was very welcome, and we just sat there and took in the wonderful view. The heavy breakers of the Indian Ocean pounded the reef edge some 600 feet away from where we sat. At any minute we expected to see footprints in the sand and man Friday appearing out of the trees. It really was an idyllic setting with not another person in sight. Even the resident local Maldivians rarely visited this stretch of beach which was covered in large and small shells of every description as well as the odd body of a crab or crayfish that had probably been some reef dweller's breakfast. It seemed to us that it was even desecration just to walk on the beach which had probably remained in its present state for a great many years and had only been re-sculpted by the action of the wind and waves. It was utter peace and tranquillity.

By this time we had both been out in the sun for nearly five hours and were getting hungry. Stupidly neither of us had brought along a drink so we decided to return along the beach to the transmitter station. Our shoulders were now feeling decidedly sore and the thought of a cool beer drove us on even faster.

We arrived back at the transmitter station and Trevor the cook, who was now working his monthly stint as the resident cook on Hithadhoo, put together omelette and chips for us. This was supplemented by a couple of cans of Red Barrel and our day was complete.

I caught the evening Pinnace back to Gan and later on, after just a little more liquid refreshment, had the best night's sleep I had had for many years.

The Weather

October's weather was, to say the least, changeable. The early part of the month was a mix of sunshine and showers with the latter being mainly at night. On the 16th it rained and kept on raining. We had 8½ inches of rain in just 12 hours and everywhere was flooded again. The heavy rain eventually gave up on the 26th of the month and it then turned very hot again. The temperature in our billet in the evening with the fan going full blast was 85°F and outside it was a moonlight and starlight night. By the end of the month it was 90°F in the billet and 115°F on the veranda just outside our room during the day. There were not many takers for the tennis courts.

The Island Club

Our WVS worker Miss June Caton has been interviewed on Radio Gan by Trevor, about her objectives for the Island Club. She said she didn't really feel lonely on Gan and did not want another woman to help her. She was very busy organising tournaments for table tennis, snooker, tennis, and darts, every week. She ate all her meals in the Officers' Mess. Umm!

Chuff Factor

315 days now completed, with 50 to do, my "chuff factor" was beginning to take off.

NOVEMBER

The month began with a bang on the 5th in traditional celebration of Guy Fawkes' attempt to blow up the Houses of Parliament. There was a fireworks display at the NAAFI at 2000 hrs which was followed by a talent contest and a barbecue. We broadcast the talent contest over Radio Gan so those unable to get to the NAAFI could at least have some idea as to just what they were missing and to have the odd laugh or two at, or admiration for, some of the contestants' efforts.

The weather was kind throughout the evening and the contest went off without a hitch. One of the stars of the evening was "Woody" from the marine section. He really was a very talented piano player in his own right as well as being the accompanist for many of the other contestants. Everyone had a really great time.

Bad News

My next posting came through early in November and it was to number 14 Maintenance Unit at RAF Stafford. Some 4000 people worked on the site but the majority of them were civilians. I was to work on radio vehicles installing new equipment or servicing old.

I was certainly not very happy at this posting as I felt that with my specialised knowledge of the IAL equipment and my unique experience of operating it, that my talents could more usefully be employed elsewhere. New IAL equipment was being delivered to many RAF sites throughout the world, but none for RAF Stafford.

Although disappointed with the news, I thought that as I only had 7 months of my National Service to do that I would make the most of the situation and not push my luck. After all I had been very fortunate up to now knowing that, even before doing my basic training, I was going to be posted to Gan to work on my civilian employers' equipment. This was certainly not the normal National Serviceman's situation.

Phew Again

Although the weather at the start of November was changeable with some strong winds, by the middle of the month is was back to lots of sunshine, 100°F temperatures and a light breeze. It remained like this for 5 solid weeks.

Notice of Repatriation

This notice (see following page), suitably filled in, was sent back home by most airmen about one month prior to returning to the UK. It was originally produced on a Creed 7B teleprinter.

Reef Watch

Throughout my eleven months on Gan hardly a day had been missed when I had not been snorkelling over the reef. My fascination for this most pleasurable of pastimes had not diminished in the least with time and as my tour was now nearing its end I felt that I should make one last effort in trying to record on film the beauty of the reef and all its inhabitants.

I certainly could not afford an underwater camera so I decided that the next best solution was to fit a Perspex panel into the bottom of a canoe and take photographs through it. One of the airmen who had left Gan recently had been very active during his stay and built a canoe which he had given to the lads in the Comms section. We all agreed that it would not detract from the canoe's sea worthiness if we did fit a viewing panel and would help other users to get some reef shots with their cameras.

The panel was fitted, no leaks were found and I took the canoe out over the reef. The biggest problem that I found was trying to ensure that the camera was in focus. In spite of having a single lens reflex camera with a ground glass screen it was extremely difficult to focus accurately. I took a number of shots and hoped for the best as I would not see the results until I returned to the UK and the film was processed.

Unfortunately the pictures I took were virtually useless. The Perspex panel filtered out the brilliant colours of the coral and all shots were out of focus. Most disappointing.

The Body in the Bath

It was now the end of November and some of the boys in our billet decided that they were going to do some serious fishing off the jetty. They specifically wanted to catch a shark, which I guess is most anglers' dream, so they took some very heavy line and some really high and foul smelling meat thrown out from the Airmen's Mess as bait. I think they were all a little surprised when after about 30 minutes of fishing they hooked what was obviously a very large fish.

After a considerable struggle they were even more surprised to see a 6 foot shark on the end of their line. They landed it and, after it eventually became motionless, carried their prize back to the billet. Someone then suggested that they should put it in one of the baths in the shower room. This they did and someone filled the bath with water.

This was definitely a bad mistake as the shark rapidly recovered and continued to lash around in the bath for the next couple of hours. By this time all the water in the bath had been displaced and the shark eventually succumbed. There was quite a reluctance to enter the bathroom for a considerable time.

The body was eventually moved from the bath and taken to the Airmen's Mess where it was prepared for part of the next days' evening meal. The Shark steak fillets were very tasty and had a texture somewhere between chicken and beef.

The only sad part to this story was the fact that when they came to cut up the shark in the mess they discovered that it was a pregnant female whose young were very well developed and would almost certainly have been born very shortly.

The Visit

The end of the month was one for a number of visits. Peter Whitcher from the MOD arrived on Gan to ascertain just how the IAL desk and equipment was working. Peter was the MOD representative responsible for the development and manufacturing contract originally awarded to IAL. He stayed on the island for only 3 days, drafted his report and returned to the UK. It was very gratifying that he found no major problems and was very complementary as to what had been achieved.

Peter left, and was immediately replaced by another inspection team lead by Sq. Ldr. Hall. This team had a broader brief than Peters' and had to assess the efficiency of all the communications equipment, not just IAL's.

Sq. Ldr. Hall asked me if I knew my posting yet as he was well aware as to just why I had been posted to Gan and what I had been doing. When I told him it was to RAF Stafford, he hit the roof and immediately sent a signal to say I was to go to RAF Stanbridge or to Signals Command at RAF Medmenham. I thanked him for his concern and he said he could not make any promises in terms of getting my posting changed, but would certainly try.

On Television (nearly)

Just before the end of November, Miss Jo Douglas, of *Six Five Special* fame came out to Gan with a camera crew to make a film for Christmas for ITV. The film was to be shown on Christmas Day and her visit was just one of a number being made to RAF stations throughout the world to give service personnel the opportunity of wishing those back home a Happy Christmas.

Bob and I were filmed dinghy sailing in the lagoon but our pictures obviously landed up on the cutting room floor as we did not appear in the finished programme.

Departure Date

The month ended and I was informed that I was scheduled to return to the UK, Lyneham, on flight USB 055 by Britannia on the 18th December. The journey would take two days. Knowing just how many times Britannias went U/S at Gan, made me just a little sceptical that I would indeed leave on that date.

DECEMBER

Early December's weather was great in spite of the fact that the average rainfall for the Maldives is 60 inches and during my stay on Gan we had had just over 100 inches of rain. I spent every spare minute of my time swimming and snorkelling on the reef making sure my tan was up to the required standard before returning home. Most evenings were spent at the Radio Gan studios where I handed over the reins of technical responsibility for the station to my successor, Corporal Bob Leisk.

Problem Comet

There was an incident on the 7th when a Comet aircraft, which had left early in the morning for Aden, had to return to Gan because of suspected undercarriage problems. It was fully expected that the undercarriage would collapse on landing, so full emergency procedures were rapidly put into place.

There were many families, including children, on board returning to the UK for Christmas. The aircraft made a low level pass over the control tower so the controllers could try to ascertain the nature of the problem and the position of the undercarriage. After going around once more the aircraft made a normal approach and thankfully landed safely. There were certainly many relieved faces.

Good News

As it was now just a week to my scheduled return to the UK. I had given up any hope of hearing any news about a change in my posting. I was still working days at the CCS/Receiver station and out of the blue I received a telephone call from one of the lads and Radio Gan colleague, who worked in the Commcen. He thought that I may be interested to know that he had just seen a signal which indicated that my posting in the UK had been changed and I was to go to RAF Stanbridge. I thanked him most sincerely for this very welcome news and awaited apprehensively for the signal to reach me via official channels. This it did about an hour later through WO Marsh.

The news was particularly pleasing as RAF Stanbridge was where the next IAL equipment was already being fitted and even more pleasing was the fact that, Stanbridge was only seven miles from my home. How lucky can you get?

Party Time

It was certainly now a time for celebrations. WO Marsh, who arrived on Gan with me and had been our boss over the last year, had his going away party at the CCS/Receiver building on the evening of the 8th. He insisted that he would pay for absolutely everything and would not accept contributions from anyone. This was very typical of this well liked and generous man.

It certainly was a party to be remembered and was crowned by Seamus, our tame Irishman, deciding that he was going to ride his bicycle around the top of the retaining wall of the static water tank.

This task would be pretty difficult even in a sober state, let alone after drinking a considerable amount of beer. To give him his due he did manage to complete one full circumnavigation of the tank but then fell headlong, complete with bicycle, into the water. This did little to deter our Seamus and he remounted his bike, under the water, and continued to pedal around the water tank until the effort just became too much.

We pulled him out, laid him down and he went to sleep, as the photographic evidence reveals.

Leaving parties became the order of the day. There was mine, Harry's, Colin and Dave's, Trevor's and many more. The alcoholic haze just did not seem to clear away.

Departure Time

On the 14th December I wrote my last letter home and completed packing ready for my departure on the 18th.

Crowning Glory

The day before I was scheduled to leave was a Saturday and I decided to get up very early and have a final snorkel over the reef. There had been a little rain overnight which had now stopped and the sun was up and it was going to be yet another very hot day. The lagoon was just like a millpond and the water was absolutely crystal clear. I waded into the water at the usual point just by the Officers' Mess.

I donned my snorkel and what met my eyes was one of the most magnificent underwater scenes I had ever witnessed. Wherever you looked on the reef there were shoals of brilliantly coloured fish. Not just the usual groups of twenty or thirty fish but literally hundreds of fish of every shape, size and colour. As I swam towards each group in turn they parted like the opening curtains of a theatre and then, when I had passed the curtain closed behind me once again. Why so many fish had gathered in this one spot I did not know. I thought it may be because a large predator like a shark was in the area but I certainly did not see anything to cause any concern. I swam amongst these fish for nearly two hours and also paid the resident Moray eel one last visit before departing the sea for the last time. It was an extremely humbling experience.

Goodbye Gan

My scheduled Britannia did arrive the next day on time and just for a nice change it did not go unserviceable as many before had done. I said goodbye to Mohammed, my very faithful room boy and to the other lads in the billet who still had some time to do and to all my friends at Radio Gan.

I left Gan with very mixed feelings. On the positive side I was going home to be with all my friends and family again and to spend a traditional Christmas in front of a log fire. On the negative side I was having to leave all my service colleagues and good friends made during my year long tour on the island. My association with Radio Gan was coming to an end. I was also having to leave a tropical island which was surrounded by some of the most spectacular living coral reefs and marine life in the world and which I had been very privileged to see and albeit briefly, be a part of.

As the Britannia took off and we flew over the western end of the runway I could see the roof of billet 47 which had been my home for much of my stay and I wondered if I would ever return to this paradise island in the Indian Ocean.

Home at Last

I arrived back in the UK at RAF Lyneham on 20th December. Customs here charged me what seemed like a fortune on the presents I had bought in Changi, but they still worked out very much cheaper than if I had bought them in the UK.

I left Lyneham by coach and then caught the train home. I have never felt so cold in all my life. There had been severe frosts in the UK at night and snow had fallen and covered many of the hills. The train journey home seemed to take forever but I eventually made it to Apsley station, near Hemel Hempstead. I left my kit at the station, to be picked up later, and walked the 1½ miles home. I arrived mid afternoon and gave Mum quite a shock and pleasant surprise as she was not expecting me. There were tears of joy as she became accustomed to having a native Maldivian living in her midst. It was great to be home just in time to celebrate Christmas with all my family.

RAF Gan 1960. WO Marsh's leaving party.
He's the one with a tie.

NOTICE OF REPATRIATION

Issued in solemn warning this *16th day of November 1960* to the parents, wives, friends and relatives of:

Number *5070684* Rank *J/T* Name ***Butler M***

Precautions before arrival

1. Stock up your fridge with plenty of beer and spirits, as this will have been his staple diet for the past eleven months.

2. Chop up all fire wood and get in coal, as any temperature below 75 degrees f is cold to him and temperatures below 60 degrees f. Are freezing.

3. Refrain from asking him what it is like in the Far East Air Force, as you may receive more in his reply than you bargained for.

Treatment after arrival

The above named airman will once more come into your presence dehydrated, decomposed and thoroughly demoralised, to take up a somewhat delayed pursuit of happiness. In making preparations for his return you are advised to make allowances for the crude environment and extreme poverty which has surrounded his life for the past eleven months. In all probability he will be suffering from a certain kind of lunacy known as "Ganitus" and therefore it will be advisable to keep him away from the sun for several weeks.

During the next six months (the usual time for a F.E.A.F. Airman to return to normal), be especially watchful when he is in the company of women, especially young and beautiful women. It must be explained that his intentions are sincere but will be extremely dishonourable. Treat him with kindness, tolerance and vast quantities of beer, wines, spirits, alka-seltzers, food, cigarettes and money. Then the true ***Michael*** you once knew will eventually emerge from the hollow shell he is in at the present.

Never laugh at him when he does something that seems stupid to you, or he will take reprisals saying "there laugh that off." Generally speaking, except for a grunt and a tendency to leap about yelling strange words, he will be comparatively calm. You are advised to show no signs of alarm if he prefers to squat on his haunches instead of sitting in a chair, pours gravy over his dessert, mixes fish with custard and insists on taking off his shoes before entering the house. For several weeks he will want to sleep with no clothes on and walk about with only a towel about his middle and 'flip-flops' (a form of oriental footwear). be patient when he takes his mattress off his bed and puts it on the floor to sleep on. There is no doubt he will mutter such unintelligible words as "salamat malam" for good evening, but in a relatively short time he will be able to read, write and even speak English again.

Probably the most important points to remember are:
– never ask him why the chap down the road has a higher rank than him.
– never make complimentary remarks about the Army, Navy and especially the Air Force in his presence.

Finally, never speak about the mystic or mysterious orient to him, or he will probably enlighten you with what it is really like out here, which believe me, will be quite a mouthful.

You have been warned.

COUNCIL FOR THE REPATRIATION OF AIRMEN

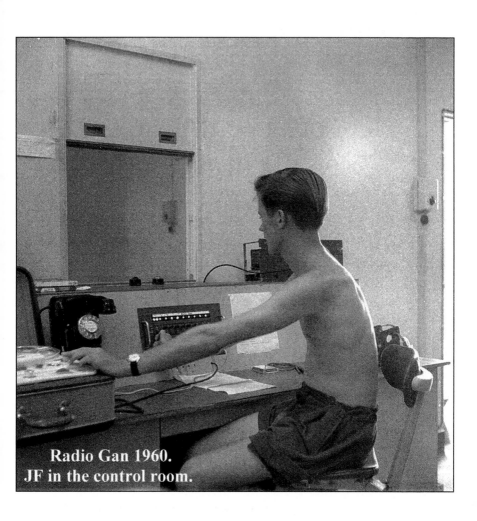

**Radio Gan 1960.
JF in the control room.**

The Radio Gan Story

Radio Gan was born out of necessity. With about 450 men on the island in January 1960 there was little to do other than the routine work associated with an RAF staging post. Leisure time facilities were strictly limited. There was of course the NAAFI Club where billiards, snooker and table tennis could be played. The club also provided snack meals, sandwiches and soft drinks throughout the day and its bar was open each evening. There was also the Astra cinema where the films were changed every two days and a floodlit tennis court for the really energetic.

For some people these facilities were sufficient but I, like the majority on the island, soon became bored with our leisure time especially after the sun went down. At least during the day you could go swimming and snorkelling over the reef, but in the evenings you were limited to the foregoing facilities or your pit.

I suppose that it was a fairly obvious move that as we all worked for the Comms section during the day then we should be the ones to launch a radio station.

The priority was therefore for sufficient money to purchase all the necessary equipment or to appropriate it from sources not necessarily to be disclosed.

Sq. Ldr Murray, who was in charge of the Commcen, asked me if I could look around for a suitable transmitter. He knew that I had been working at the transmitter site at Hithadhoo with Neil Drayfus and Chris Robinson the Marconi installation and commissioning team.

Neil came up trumps with a 1 Kilowatt transmitter which Marconi had used for inter-island communication prior to more permanent channels being established and which was no longer required. It was going to be dumped over the reef so we saved it from an early grave.

It was just what we were looking for and was designed to radiate on a frequency of 1.2 MHz in the medium waveband. I seem to remember that Neil also found us some spare valves to keep it running.

Sq. Ldr Murray in the meantime had been in contact with the "Nuffield" organisation and they had promised us £250 as an initial donation to buy some equipment, then further funding per month for records or other equipment as we became established.

Other lads in the Radio Gan team had chatted up the resident Shackleton Search and Rescue crews with a view to getting them to buy us equipment in Singapore during one of their weekly changeovers. This they willingly agreed to do and to purchase records for us on a regular basis.

To supplement the transmitter which had now been shipped to Gan from Hithadhoo much searching uncovered an ancient tape recorder complete with microphone and a turntable.

We borrowed these items from their current owners and installed them with the transmitter in a spare room at the end of the Commcen. We persuaded one of the Maldivian room boys to shin up a pair of conveniently placed palm trees just outside the Commcen to fix the transmitter aerial.

"On the Air"

It was now early February and we all decided that our first broadcast would take place on Saturday 13th. It was our intention to put out the "Top Twenty" which some kind soul had recorded on tape for us and, if possible, to re-broadcast the football results straight from the BBC in London.

Initially I had the job as disc jockey and chief announcer and with our very crude set-up we first tested live on Wednesday evening the 10th February. Nothing blew up and a quick check with our team sporting their portable radios confirmed that we could be heard loud and clear throughout the island. Our contacts on Hithadhoo confirmed that their reception was also OK.

Saturday evening arrived and at 1830 hrs, I, their very first and very nervous announcer, launched the first broadcast of Radio Gan. Fortunately everything went without a hitch and at least I did not get tongue tied. We had only a very small number of records available so our early broadcasts did not run very long. We thought we had done quite well if we could broadcast for a couple of hours without a break.

We all took turns at being the resident disc jockey and announcer and such was our success that the NAAFI shop soon sold out of radios.

At the end of February the Search and Rescue crew coming in from Singapore delivered the first of our new equipment. This consisted of a Grundig tape recorder, two transcription turntables, a good quality studio microphone and about 25 records as well as some blank tapes.

It very soon became apparent to all of us that what we really required in terms of accommodation for Radio Gan was not one room but two. One room as the studio and the other as a control room. After a certain amount of boot licking we were given the adjoining rooms at the end of the Commcen. These were ideal as there was a small hatch in the wall dividing the rooms. The wooden hatch was soon removed and replaced with two large sheets of perspex well spaced so as to provide good sound insulation.

The end room became the studio which was made acoustically dead by hanging bed blankets down the wall and an "On Air" light was attached to the door.

We also decided that with the new equipment the turntables would be mounted on a desk in the studio but the control of their motors should be exercised from the control room. This meant the announcer set the records up on the turntable and the controller determined their start and connection on air. This meant we all had to learn the art of backtracking records so the record was just up to speed as the track started.

If there was one thing we were not short of on the island, it was wooden packing cases and both the studio and control room desks were quickly made from them.

The only device we could find that could be adapted as a control panel for turntables, microphone and tape recorder was a AD2641,

10 line Post Office switchboard. This was ideal as each key switch position had a red and white light associated with it. The white light we used to indicate standby mode and the red light indicated "on air".

By the middle of March all the new kit, including the much modified control switchboard, was in place and our recruitment drive to obtain new announcers and controllers was bearing fruit.

We also decided that our opening signature tune would be Tommy Dorsey playing "Song of India" by Nikolae Rimsky-Korsakov. Others in our group were now busily working out programme schedules for the coming weeks and persuading people to put together and present a half-hour's programme to help fill it. The decision was also made that we would broadcast from 0600 to 0700 hrs in the morning and from 1800 to 2315 hrs in the evening.

On the evening of Sunday 3rd April 1960 Radio Gan went into full swing and we were now fully committed to providing our listeners with a regular broadcasting service.

I decided that my announcer non-de-plume was to be Richard Michelmore. What a mouthful.

Outside Broadcasts

By the end of April we were asked if we could make use of a pair of walkie-talkies. As the technical authority for Radio Gan I quickly accepted these on Radio Gan's behalf and asked no further questions as to where they had come from. The Army lads had left anyway. They were absolutely ideal for outside broadcasts and we quickly put them to good use going around the billets getting people to say a few words on air about their time on Gan, what they did and then playing a record of their choice. This became quite a popular programme as quite a few interviewed on air did not hesitate in saying *exactly* what they thought of the place.

Bleeper Required

An incident occurred one evening with Trevor and Peter when opening the radio station. These two lads were very new to Radio Gan, as we all were, and were always a little apprehensive when their turn came to manning the station. Trevor was the controller and Peter was the announcer.

Trevor was always pretty reserved and never got very worried about anything in particular. Peter, on the other hand was always very twitchy and nervous about most things and really was the biggest hypochondriac I have ever met. He seemed to be always reporting sick to the MO for the most insignificant of things. If it wasn't a sore throat then it would be a mozzie-bite or some other totally insignificant problem. However, this particular evening, they had arrived at the studio with only about five minutes to go before the scheduled "On Air" opening time.

In order to fully appreciate what happened next it is necessary to understand a little about the technical operation of Radio Gan. The studio was fitted with the two transcription turntables and the desk microphone for the announcer. The announcer had to wear a pair of earphones in order to hear exactly what was going "out on air," and for communication with the controller next door. The announcer also had the task of back-tracking the records placed on the turntables so that the table itself was up to speed before the record began. Control of the turntable motors rested with the controller next door. The controller's other task was to switch on the microphone when required by the announcer. When the microphone was not being used for an "On Air" announcement it was used so that the controller and announcer could communicate with each other. A large red light on the top of the control desk indicated when the microphone was live and "on air" and this was clearly visible to both announcer and controller. An "On Air" light on the outside of the studio door also warned visitors not to enter.

The Radio Gan signature tune record was duly placed on one of the turntables by Peter and the follow-up record on the other. The appointed start-up time had arrived and Trevor initiated turntable one. Unfortunately, Peter had incorrectly back-tracked the record and it started with a crescendo whine. It was made even worse by the fact that the turntable had its speed set to 78 rpm instead of 45 rpm required for our signature tune record. At this stage it was Trevor who panicked first by running around from the control room to the studio and adjusting the turntable speed whilst the record was still going out on air. Peter by this time had now dropped the evening's programme schedule on the floor and was frantically trying to retrieve it before the signature tune stopped. He managed to do this just in time and after a very hesitant start, read out just what was in store for the listeners that evening. The next record was then started.

In was then that, over the top of this record, the never forgotten words were heard:

"Cor Trev, that was a f—ing good start to the evening, can we try again?"

Trevor, unfortunately, had left Peter's studio microphone switched "on air".

I had just about returned to my billet after setting up the Radio Gan transmitter and was listening on my portable. I have never heard so much laughter in all my life. The whole island seemed to burst with laughter with great guffaws coming from each and every billet and much banging on billet walls and beds.

It seems that amongst their listeners was the RAF Padre who was not in the slightest bit amused by the language and went out of his way to ensure that his feelings were known by all, especially Radio Gan announcers. Our listening audience greatly increased after this incident. I suppose everyone was waiting for something like it to happen again, but of course it didn't.

BBC or Bust

It was decided that, as it was almost impossible to pick up the overseas service from the BBC on a small portable radio, we should re-broadcast their transmission over Radio Gan. With suitable permission from the Warrant Officer in charge of the CCS and

Receiver station, it was agreed that we could use a spare receiver and aerials and connect the audio output over the land lines to the Commcen and into Radio Gan. The only problem was that there were no cables between the Commcen and the Radio Gan control room over which we could send these signals. In a moment of sheer stupidity I volunteered to fit the extra cable.

This seemed a fairly simple task and we were given permission to use the roof space in the Commcen through which to route the new cable. I soon found a suitable roof access point in the Commcen and with a leg-up from the other lads got into the roof space area. It was at this point that I realised my mistake. All the later buildings on Gan had corrugated iron roofs and the building ceilings were very well insulated by thick mats of insulating material. The temperature in the sun outside was probably 130°F and the temperature in the roof space was, well, *very very* hot indeed to say the least. You just could not touch the inside of the corrugated roof panels at all or you would have been badly burnt. This environment had absolutely nothing on even the hottest sauna that is imaginable.

I told the lads down below as to what it was like and that if I did not reappear after ten minutes then they would have to come up and drag me out. The cable run was probably only about 20 yards, but it did mean traversing at least two fire barrier partitions. These are built at regular intervals throughout the length of the roof to act as fire retardant barriers and each had a small boltable door so as to allow access between the sections. I eventually managed to route the cable to a ceiling tile over the Radio Gan control room, made a hole, and passed the cable through to one of the boys down below. I then beat a hasty retreat to the roof access point in the Commcen, making certain to bolt the access doors on the roof partitions behind me.

Descending into the air conditioned 75°F of the Commcen felt like going inside the ice making compartment of a fridge and I just had to go into the cool air and 100°F+ shade temperatures outside. The lads I must say were very complimentary about my efforts and after I had taken a well earned shower, took me to the NAAFI for a "tinny" or three, I certainly needed it. I must have lost pounds. I was very glad that the cable we put in was a multiple pair type as we used this for carrying both audio and dc signals to run a teleprinter.

By early May we were re-broadcasting the overseas service of the BBC on a regular basis using the newly laid cable connected back to a receiver at the CCS/Receiver building. We also managed to borrow a teleprinter for use in the control room and connected this to a news FSK transmission from Reuters, via the same route, so as to obtain the UK football results as well as other interesting items of news. We usually managed to get the results off the printer and broadcast over Radio Gan before the BBC's Vidiprinter had even started. What a good job that Reuters did not know or we may have been in trouble.

The Radio Gan staff count had now gone up to 35 people. This meant that my services and others in the team, as announcer or controller were only required about twice during a week of broadcasting. It certainly eased the enormous pressure we all felt during the very early days and weeks of Radio Gan when there were only about six of us to do everything.

Top Team Quiz

One of our converts to Radio Gan was the education officer. He agreed to set a series of general knowledge questions to be answered by teams of four people representing the various work sections on the island. He would be the question master.

The problem was that the studio was not large enough to accommodate more than three people let alone two four man teams and the education officer.

This problem was solved when we were given the use of one of the spare rooms in one of the billets. Here it was possible to house teams, question master, announcer and a limited audience of about 20 people. It was certainly quite a squash with everyone in but, with an audience, added considerably to the atmosphere of the programme. The other problem was that the billet did not have air conditioning so after thirty minutes on air, it got rather warm, especially as we had to acoustically dampen the room by hanging blankets down the walls. The problem was always helped by having copious supplies of drink on hand.

Connection of the audio feed from the billet back to the studio was achieved by routing the signals over the island's telephone system. It meant tying up a line and two phones throughout the transmission of the programme but we did not receive any complaints. We used this same method for transmissions from the NAAFI when it was required to broadcast talent contests, musical evenings, etc. If a phone was not easily accessible then we used the walkie-talkies to provide a radio link.

Far and Wide

Shortly after Radio Gan became established in April we asked everyone listening if they would inform their families and friends back in the UK that we would like to run a "record request from home" programme and write directly to Radio Gan, BFPO 180. We had to say that as our record collection was limited then we may have to substitute the music requested with something which we judged to be near that asked for.

It was not very long before the messages and requests began arriving from home and wherever possible we informed the nominated recipient when the request was to be broadcast. We also tried to agree with the listener an alternative record if the one asked for was not in our library.

We soon had enough requests coming in to run a regular half hour programme at least twice a week.

One thing did surprise us however and that was the fact that we started to receive requests for RAF servicemen stationed in Eastleigh, South Africa, and in Singapore. We then learnt that Radio Gan was being regularly picked up in both these locations. We were told that, although our signals were not brilliant, that under certain atmospheric conditions that we could be heard quite well and RAF staff and their families were enjoying our programmes.

This news generated a certain amount of anxiety amongst our staff, not least amongst some of our announcers, who, up to now, thought they had a limited audience restricted to the Addoo Atoll. With this knowledge in hand we all redoubled our efforts to ensure that another "Pete and Trev" incident did not occur, especially as there could be children amongst our listeners.

We eventually won over the Padre who agreed to present a half-hour service each Sunday evening which was very well received by everyone. We also provided air time for the Pakistani contingent on the island and broadcast a pre-recorded religious programme for them on a regular basis.

Bunny

Once in a while one comes across one of those larger than life characters who once seen are never forgotten. Bunny, as he was affectionately known, was such a character. He walked into the Radio Gan studio one evening, luckily the "On Air" red light was off and offered his services in preparing and presenting an hour's long programme on classical music. We were obviously apprehensive about this since we had no idea what he intended to do and could only make a guess at the audience reaction which would follow. At this particular time we were short of programme material so we accepted his kind offer and waited for his first offering the following Sunday. He suggested the programme should be called "Bunny's Choice".

Bunny, at a guess, was in his late fifties and worked for the Air Ministry Works Department, AMWD for short. He sported a large slightly ginger bushy beard and always wore the regulation AMWD clothes. These consisted of khaki shorts, short sleeved shirt, long socks and some highly polished black shoes. Bunny was always immaculately turned out, went everywhere in his jeep and commanded great respect from all who worked for him in AMWD. This included local Maldivians as well as expatriate staff.

Bunny, who was very articulate, had two main passions in his life. One was his obvious love and passion for all types of classical music. He had the largest audio system set up in his living quarters that one could imagine coupled with a considerable selection of classical records. Second was his love of good food and alcoholic beverages, especially whisky. He had two local Maldivians who looked after him. One looked after Bunny's accommodation and served all his meals and the other was his cook. He put great demands on both of them and often complained that they were not up to his usual standard. In spite of this they were extremely loyal and made every effort to please him.

Bunny's knowledge of classical music was extraordinary. Each composer's life history and the music that each wrote could be recalled in the smallest detail. He could produce information covering the very oldest to the present day composers. He also had a natural ability to impart his fund of knowledge in a most interesting and effective way.

We certainly need not have worried about "Bunny's Choice". He lavishly illustrated his programme with excerpts from the classics to underline the points he was trying to make and the story he was telling. His programmes were a sheer delight. It was a great personnel tribute to his skills that many service personnel, who normally had not the slightest interest in classical music, would listen avidly to his programme each Sunday night.

In spite of the very professional presentation given by Bunny, he did indicate to us that he was extremely nervous in front of the microphone. This was especially so when he learnt that our audience extended to Singapore and Eastleigh. To overcome his little problem he usually brought a bottle of whisky and suitably large glass to the studio for each broadcast. "Just to calm the nerves", as he would say. By the end of each programme his enthusiasm for his music and the whisky was at its peak and every broadcast was a resounding success. He often overran his allotted sixty minutes but no one worried about this. He certainly did not mind, especially if there was a drop left in the bottle. We did however have to drive him back to his accommodation on more that one occasion. His faithful servant would then help put him to bed for a well earned rest. Next morning Bunny would be up early, as usual, sporting a freshly laundered and immaculately pressed set of regulation tropical clothes. What a character.

Gilding the Lily

Radio Gan was, by June 1960, a resounding success. We had a very loyal local and overseas audience. We had sufficient contributors and presenters to fill our programme schedules for weeks to come as well as a regular band of announcers and controllers to present the programmes. It was also very gratifying to find that new personnel arriving on the island did not take much coaxing to join our staff. The future of the station seemed assured.

I, however, had been conscious for some time that the technical facilities at Radio Gan were not as good as they should or could be and it was in my court as the technical authority to do something about it. Our operation was very "digital". Records were either on or off as was the microphone with no way of fading or mixing them. The tape recorder did have a line output control but this was of limited use.

I therefore wrote to a colleague, who worked at my previous employers as an electronic design engineer. I outlined the problem and asked if he could come up with the design for a relatively simple ten channel audio fader and mixing unit. This he very quickly did and I further imposed on him to obtain all the necessary components from the company through their staff sale scheme, as it would be much cheaper that buying from a shop and then to ship them out to me.

It was early August when all the new kit arrived and a group of four of us set to work making up ten identical audio modules that would form the basis of the ten channel fader and mixer unit. Obtaining the sheet aluminium to make the chassis was not a problem as it was available from the lads in the aircraft servicing section. What was a problem was finding suitable sizes and numbers of nuts, bolts, washers and screws to mount such items such as valveholders, terminal blocks, etc.

Many hours were spent rummaging through boxes of spares before we had sufficient to complete the job. I seem to remember one or two spare radio units may have had a couple of screws that went missing. Trying to build electronic kit with the nearest shop some 2,500 miles away was not easy and resourcefulness had therefore to play its part.

By mid August the new equipment was completed and tests performed in standalone form suggested it was doing exactly what it was designed to do.

There was now just one problem. In order to install the new equipment we were going to have to do the previously unthinkable. We were going to have to shut down Radio Gan. We were off the air from 15th August to our Grand Gala Re-opening on 28th August. Everyone was soon asking when we were going to be back again.

We took the opportunity when installing the new equipment to tidy up all the original wiring and to revamp both studio and announcer's desks to simplify operations and make accommodation more comfortable. We also made housing for the 220 records now in our library and indexed them all for easy access. It was very hard work but well worth the effort.

One of the results of us being off the air was that NAAFI club sales of food and especially drink increased considerably.

The evening of Sunday 28th August arrived and with quite a large amount of trepidation we went back on the air. The script for the first 10 minutes of the programme was as follows:-

RADIO GAN AT WORK

FADE IN SOUND OF SAWS, HAMMERS, BRUMMAGUM SCREWDRIVERS, ETC.

Dramatis Personae:
Alfie Crudd, a technician
Mick Butler, his stooge
Bob Leisk, A general handyman
Doug Greenland, a librarian who doubles on the screwdriver
Brian Flatt, a set square.

Crudd	"Ere Mick, what time did he say we're going on the air?
Mick	6.30 wasn't it?
Bob	That's right, 6.30 it was.
Crudd	We're a bit pushed then. Give us a hand to push this desk back.

(Grunts and noises as desk is shifted)

Bob	How's that?
Mick	*(gently)* There is just one thing wrong with it.
Bob	What?
Mick	*(loudly)* It's on my flipping toe!!
Crudd	Sorry. It's your own fault for wearing flip flops. *(Sound of desk being moved again)* That's better? Right, let's fix it to the wall *(noise of screwdrivers)*. Where's Doug?
Doug	*(voice muffled)* I'm under here.
Mick	Under where?
Doug	Under the desk. I'm just fixing this speaker.
Mick, Crudd & Bob *in unison*	Oh No!
Bob	Clot! We've just fixed that to the wall.
Doug	Well, just unfix it. I want to get out.
Mick	No time now, we're on the air in a few minutes. We'll let you out when we go over to the BBC.
Doug	*(Goonish voice)* You dirty rotten swine. You have shutted me in!
Crudd	Shut up and tell us if all the valves light up when we switch on.

Mick	I reckon we are about set for testing now. Let's try everything.
Bob	Alfie, you go in the studio and slap some records on. I'll switch on. Contact!
Doug	YEOUWWWWW!!!
Mick	Well, the mains is getting through anyway. OK Doug?
Doug	I guess so. I can manage without that finger.
Bob	Ready Alfie?
Crudd	OK here.
Bob	Check mic volume control. Say something.
Crudd	There was a young man of Calcutta, who was having... *(Fade)*
Mick	That's fading OK. Bring it up again.
Crudd	*(Fade in)* ... in the gutter. OK?
Bob	Wizard. Now turntable one. *(Fade in tune 1)*
Bob	Cut to number two.

(Fade in tune 2. They fade these tunes in and out for a bit then fade.)

Mick	Now bring up the tape recorder *(plays at slow speed)*. Something wrong there. Doug!
Doug	*(still muffled)* Whatsamatter?
Mick	Take out V2 in Amp 1.
Doug	OK OWWWW!!!!
Crudd	Was it hot?
Doug	I'll say it was.
Crudd	Put it back then. It can't be that one.
Bob	Hang on. I think I can fix it. *(Bang, crash, bash etc.)* Try it now.

(Tape comes up OK. Sax, sex and song or Charles and Bassett, in fact anything but Gan at Work!)

Mick   No, not that! Turn it off!

(Cut tape)

Crudd   Well, that's about it. Just in time. Two minutes to go.

Bob   I'll put the transmitter on.

(Enter Brian)

Brian   Good evening. What's going on?

ALL   Good evening.

Mick   It's all tested. We're just ready to go on the air.

Brian   I've got news for you. You've been on the air for the last ten minutes.

ALL WHAT!!

Silence, followed by "Song of India" and usual programmes...

Radio Gan was back!

All Sorts

Although Radio Gan's staff consisted of Officers, Sergeants, Corporals and Airmen of all ranks as well as some civilian staff, no one tried to pull rank and we all used to work together on an equal basis, usually on Christian name terms. I am sure this attitude was responsible for establishing Radio Gan as an institution which would last for many years.

It was September and I now had my own hour long programme on Sunday evening called "Classical Hour". This was not too difficult to do as I just selected the classical music that I really liked and played it over the air. It was probably my programme that prompted "Bunny" to come along to our studio and offer his services. He certainly made his programme far more interesting than mine.

Out of Sorts

In early June, I, or my controller, Jack Findlay, had the pleasure of recording the Pakistani Padre each Friday morning. This usually consisted of one half-hour of chants and wailing with the programme going out on air each Friday afternoon. It certainly wasn't Jack's or my "Top of the Pops".

Our Pakistani friends were very appreciative that we did this. They were so grateful that that they bought us a bottle of whisky as a thank-you present. They, of course, as devout Muslims, did not drink. Jack and I were invited to their camp and arrived there early one evening by bicycle, we were then plied with the whisky, neat.

We did not want to offend them, so proceeded slowly to consume the complete bottle. Needless to say we were very merry when we left some three hours later. The only thing I do remember about our journey back to our billets in the pitch black, was falling off my bike at least three or four times near the end of the runway and landing up in a monsoon ditch. I also seem to remember, unsuccessfully, trying to ride up "Mount Gan". This was a 5 foot pile of earth near the end of the runway.

The next day we both had massive hangovers which took several more days to get rid of. We both said, "never again", but of course we did.

Best of Sorts

In October one of the Radio Gan team had plucked up courage and wrote to the BBC telling them of our radio station and of the fact that we were re-broadcasting the overseas service of the BBC and asking if they could help us with programme material of any form. We were all a bit apprehensive about the reply we would receive.

The reply was really positive and instead of receiving a rebuke we received a parcel of discs, free of charge, from the BBC's Transcription Service. These discs included "The Paul Temple

Series", (a serial), "Hancocks Half Hour", and "Round the Horn", with more to follow shortly on a regular basis.

Road's End

My year on Gan was all too quickly drawing to a close and one of my last tasks was to set up the necessary lines and equipment for broadcasting a talent contest from the NAAFI in November. It was now time to hand over the reins as technical authority to someone else. Corporal Bob Leisk took over from me in December 1960 and I left the island just before Christmas. I sent Bob a Radio Gan Christmas present from the UK in the form of a load of spares which I knew he would make good use of. In return I received a very much appreciated letter from Flt Lt Philbrick on behalf of the Radio Gan Committee thanking me for all my efforts in helping to establish the radio station.

UK Special

Shortly before returning to the UK I promised to keep in touch with the Radio Gan team and, if possible, to send out some programme material. This resulted over the first months of 1961 in the making of six half-hour programmes called "UK Special". I only achieved this with the help and assistance of my good friend Charles Hampton, the electronics engineer who had designed the ten channel audio fader and mixer which we had installed at Radio Gan.

We took turns at writing the script with each programme becoming more way out than the last. I seem to remember that Charles (alias Horace) and I (Richard) had a man in space about four weeks before the first Russian was launched into orbit. This was of course Yury Alekseyevich Gagarin who was put in orbit on the 12th April 1961 aboard Vostok 1. Now that was a coup!

Each UK Special attempted some story line with some very tenuous links into record titles which were then played to fill the programme. We both certainly spent many hours finding ways to come up with sound effects which sounded plausible when played on air as well as trying to make our hammy acting, non-hammy.

On average it took some five hours to generate the thirty minutes of programme material that was required for each programme.

We were told that the UK Special programmes were a great hit on Gan and repeated twice each week. By now I was back working at RAF Stanbridge in the UK and Charles had work and other commitments which meant UK Special number 6 was our last. We really had a great time recording them and were glad that our efforts were appreciated.

RAF Gan. 1960. The Receiver room at the CCS/Receiver Station.

Footnote

Since beginning to write about my time on Gan and about my association with Radio Gan I have learnt that Radio Gan continued to provide entertainment to RAF personnel until the island was shut down as an RAF staging post in 1976. Any Radio station that lasts nearly 16 years must have something going for it and we all owe an enormous debt of gratitude to all personnel who freely gave their time and effort in keeping it on the air.

As a way of saying thank you to the lads who worked with me on Radio Gan from January to December 1960, I list below the manning rosters which applied to some of that year. If your name appears on the list then please get in touch with me via the publishers in the UK and I will put you in touch with your other Radio Gan colleagues in the RAF in 1960. I would also like to hear from anyone who was associated with Radio Gan at anytime during their service career.

Many thanks,
Michael Butler
Radio Gan

RAF Gan. 1960. Maldivian Room Boys.

Radio Room Duty List – September 1960

1st	Emery	Davis	Clerkin
2nd	Hodgetts	Cleverly	Mullest.
3rd	Leisk	Wells	Hill
4th	Robinson	Deakin	Jeffrey
5th	Fleming	Galvin	Mokler
6th	Butler	Johnson	Honey
7th	Mathews	Maskell	Hopkins
8th	Clerkin	Medland	Emery
9th	McFarlane	Gardner	Peckham
10th	Murray	Walker	Reynolds
11th	Leisk	Wells	Hill
12th	Deakin	Robinson	Jeffrey
13th	Fleming	Galvin	Mokler
14th	Hodgetts	Cleverly	Mullest
15th	Emery	Davis	Clerkin
16th	Clerkin	Medland	Emery
17th	McFarlane	Gardner	Peckham
18th	Butler	Johnson	Honey
19th	Mathews	Maskell	Hopkins
20th	Murray	Walker	Reynolds
21st	Fleming	Galvin	Mokler
22nd	Hodgetts	Cleverly	Mullest
23rd	Deakin	Robinson	Jeffery
24th	Mathews	Maskell	Hopkins
25th	Emery	Davis	Clerkin
26th	Leisk	Wells	Hill
27th	Butler	Johnson	Honey
28th	Murray	Walker	Reynolds
29th	McFarlane	Gardner	Peckham
30th	Clerkin	Medland	Emery

Duty Crews are asked to be present at the Radio Room at least five minutes before broadcasting is due to commence.

Those personnel unable to carry out their duty please contact the undersigned in sufficient time for a stand-in to be arranged.

September 1960 (P. J. Surman)

Radio Gan: RADIO GAN CREW DUTIES

Duty List for November 1960

lst	Butler - Johnson	16th	Jefferey - Peckham
2nd	Leisk - Honey	17th	McFarlane - Gardner
3rd	Morgan - Walker	18th	Matthews - Maskell
4th	Jefferey - Peckham	19th	Medland - Davies
5th	McFarlane - Gardner	20th	Beizent - Emery
6th	Matthews - Maskell	21st	Dickinson - Hole
7th	Medland - Davies	22nd	Snelling - Argent
8th	Baigent - Emery	23rd	Clerkin - Enfield
9th	Dickinson - Hole	24th	Jones - Backhaus
10th	Snelling - Argent	25th	Morgan - Walker
11th	Clerkin - Enfield	26th	Butler - Johnson
12th	Jones - Backhaus	27th	Leisk - Honey
13th	Morgan - Walker	28th	Jefferey - Peckham
14th	Butler - Johnson	29th	McFarlane - Gardner
15th	Leisk - Honey	30th	Medland - Davies

Please let Flt Lt Surman know as early as possible if you find yourself unable to carry out the duty.

E.D. Murray, *Officer I/C Radio Gan*

Distribution

Sqn Ldr E.D Murray - O.C. C.C.G.
Flt. Lt. P. Surman
Flt. Lt. Philbrick
Radio Gan (2)
C.C.S. (2)
Airmen's Mess
Spare (3)

Radio Gan Radio Times

In order to give you a flavour of the type of programmes we broadcast I have reproduced on the next few pages a copy of the *Radio Gan Times* for the week 5th to 11th September 1960. It is just as it was issued with typing errors, omissions, etc.

MONDAY EVENING

600 PM – 615 PM	B.B.C. News.
615	– 620	Programme Parade, Film Announcements.
620	– 635	Evening Star.
635	– 650	Birthday Greetings.
650	– 715	Record Miscellany.
715	– 745	Gan Roundup – Repeat of Saturdays programme.
745	– 815	National Half-Hour.
815	– 900	My kind of Music.
900	– 915	B.B.C. News.
915	– 945	Alphabetical Discs 'A'
945	– 1015	Listeners Choice.
1015	– 1045	Appointment With Fear.
1045	– 1115	Sports Report, B.B.C. News.

CLOSE DOWN

TUESDAY EVENING

600Pm – 615 Pm	B.B.C. News.
615	– 620	Programme Parade, Film Announcements.
620	– 635	Evening Star.
635	– 650	Birthday Greetings.
650	– 720	Jazz with Andy.
720	– 805	
805	– 815	Gan at Work.
815	– 845	Star Choice.
845	– 900	Freedom of the Air.
900	– 915	B.B.C. News.
915	– 945	Charles and Bassett Show.
945	– 1045	Music in the Air.
1045	– 1115	Sports RepOrt, B.B.C. News.

CLOSE DOWN

600 PM	– 615 Pm	B.B.C. News.
615	– 620	Programme Parade, Film Announcements.
620	– 635	Evening Star
635	– 650	Birthday Greetings.
650	– 730	Musical Meanderings with Bunny.
730	– 800	Letters from Home.
800	– 830	Wednesday Serial. A Radio play.
830	– 900	Listeners Choice.
900	– 915	B.B.C. News.
915	– 1015	Everybody's Music – Richard Stratton and Bunny entertain.
1015	– 1115	B.B.C. Relay :– Forces Favourites. Sports Report. B.B.C. News.

CLOSE DOWN

THURSDAY EVENING

600PM	– 615PM	B.B.C. News.
615	– 620	Programme Parade, Film Announcements.
620	– 635	Evening Star.
635	– 650	Birthday Greetings.
650	– 700	Gan at Work. A repeat of Tuesday's programme.
700	– 730	Listeners Choice.
730	– 800	Variety Half-Hour.
800	– 830	Hospital Requests.
830	– 845	World Telegram.
845	– 900	Record Interlude.
900	– 915	B.B.C. News.
915	– 945	Show Time – Music from the Shows.
945	– 1015	South of the Border. A programme of Latin–American Music.
1015	– 1045	Playhouse.
1045	– 1115	Sports Report, B.B.C. News.

CLOSE DOWN

600PM	- 615PM	B.B.C. News.
615	- 620	Programme Parade, Film Announcements.
620	- 635	Evening Star.
635	- 650	Birthday Greetings.
650	- 700	Book Review.
700	- 730	Programme for Pakistani Listeners.
730	- 800	Jazz With Andy.
800	- 830	Listeners Choice.
830	- 900	Repeat of Wednesdays Serial Play.
900	- 915	B.B.C. News.
915 -	945	Variety Spot.
945	- 1015	Announcers Choice.
1015	- 1045	Excerpts from the Operas.
1045	- 1115	Sports Report, B.B.C. News.

CLOSE DOWN

SATURDAY EVENING

600PM	- 615PM	B.B.C. News.
615	- 620	Programme Parade, Film Announcements.
620	- 635	Evening Star.
635	- 650	Birthday Greetings.
650	- 715	Saturday Serenade - introduced by Eric Ticehurst.
715	- 745	Gan Roundup.
745	- 815	Rendezvous with the Pops, with Clifford Steel.
815	- 1120	B.B.C. Relay :- Sports Roundup. Saturday Special. B.B.C. News.
1120	- 1159	Late Night Final.

CLOSE DOWN

700AM	– 800Am	Religious Programme for Pakistani Listeners.
600PM	– 615PM	B.B.C. News.
615	– 620	Programme Parade, Film Announcements.
620	630	Birthday Greetings.
630	– 700	Charles and Bassett Show – A repeat of Tuesday's programme.
700	– 715	Programme Review and Radio Station Announcements.
715	– 730	Controllers Choice.
730	– 800	Bunny's Rarebit.
800	– 830	Four-Star Variety.
830	– 900	Some Sort of Answer. The panel will endeavour to give Some Sort of Answer to Any Sort of Question.
900	– 915	B.B.C. News.
915	– 930	The Padre.
930	– 1030	Classical Hour.
1030	– 1100	Sunday Night Special – A programme of Music and Verse.
1100	– 1115	B.B.C. News.

CLOSE DOWN

RAF Gan, 1960. Search & Rescue Shackelton from 205 Squadron, Singapore.

New NAAFI. RAF Gan. 1960.

RAF Gan. 1960. Station Headquarters.

Alex Cameron   Taff Rodgers   Jack Findlay

Roger Onward Hobart   Bob Leisk   WO Marsh
Honey

Colin Coxall   Seamus   Neil Dreyfuss

Chris Robinson   Harry Waters   Trevor Johnson

RAF Gan Personnel

Wing Commander Thomas
Our original CO (December 1959 to May 1960). A liberal
gentleman who commanded great respect and was well-liked by
everyone.

Sq. Ldr Murray. Officer in charge of the Comms section on Gan
in the early part of 1960 and who obtained the initial funding for
Radio Gan.

Flt Lt Philbrick. Officer in charge of the Comms section late 1960
to early 1961. He quickly became a great champion for Radio Gan
and gave up much of his spare time helping to run it.

Flt Lt Peter Surman. I think he worked in station HQ. He also
became a staunch ally of Radio Gan, helping especially with its
update and re-launch on 28th August 1960. His Radio Gan non-
de-plume was Brian Flatt.

WO Marsh. Warrant Officer in charge of the CCS/Receiver
station building, equipment and personnel. Great personality. You
knew exactly where you stood with him. His great claim to fame,
on Gan, was to establish the garden and grass just outside the
CCS building.

Just some of the lads that I met and worked with on Gan.

Roger Onward Hobart Honey. He had the rank of SAC. He had
signed up for 10 years (I think) and worked with me at the CCS/
Receiver station. We both arrived on Gan about the same time. We
lived in the same billet for virtually the whole of our tour.

Colin Coxall (pictured right) and *Tony* both Firemen.

Dave and *John* from the Accounts Section.

Doug Greenland and *Alfie Crudd* who all worked on Radio Gan.

Harry Waters he was a typist in HQ and *Trevor Johnson* the cook. Trevor's Radio Gan non-de-plume was Clifford Steel. We all went on leave together to Singapore.

Seamus, who was very obviously Irish and whose claim to fame was riding his bicycle around the static water tank under the water. A number of us shared a room in billet 47 with him for about three months. Difficult guy to get to know. He loved parties.

John Dodds who worked at the CCS/Receiver station and accompanied me on many snorkelling trips on and over the reef.

Taff Rogers (pictured right) who was a medic at the hospital and gave us the graphic details on what operations had been performed on the local populous.

Arnie who was a resident in my billet for the last two months of my tour.

4235328 SAC *Jack Findlay* (pictured right) who was an aerial rigger and who acted as my controller at Radio Gan. Jack and I met for a drink or two a number of times in 1961 in the UK after he and I had left the RAF. Unfortunately we then lost contact. Now in October 1999, after a period of nearly 40 years, we are in touch again thanks to an aerial riggers reunion notice that appeared in the RAFA journal "Air Mail" and the great help of the reunion organiser Eddie Edwards.

5069493 Corporal *Bob Leisk* took over from me as the technical authority at Radio Gan when I left in December 1960. Bob eventually left Gan on flight UKC 03 on 19th March 1961 and was posted to the Radio Training School at Compton Bassett. We corresponded until Bob moved to the RTS and then we lost touch. Bob also had a brother in the RAF who was doing installation work on Gan just before Bob left.

Civilians working on Gan

Neil Drafus (left) and *Chris Robinson* (right) who both worked for Marconi and were responsible for installing and commissioning many items in the receiver room within CCS and a lot of the transmitters on Hithadhoo. It was from Neil that I managed to obtain the transmitter for Radio Gan.

Alex Cameron. Alex worked for AT&E and I had known him previously in civvy street through contacts at IAL. He was responsible for installing and commissioning much of the channelling equipment's in the CCS and the Commcen. We had many a tipple together, usually his favourite drink, which was Drambuie. The hangover you get from Drambuie has to be experienced to be believed! We heard that Alex finally blotted his copybook by trying to get a considerable number of watches bought in Singapore back through the customs in UK. He was caught, heavily fined, as was his company and he lost his job as a result.

Peter Whicher who was the MOD representative for the CCS contract with IAL. He came out to Gan on a number of occasions.

Pilot Officer Williams, who was ex HQ90 Group, Signals Command, Medmenham and eventually came out to Gan for a one year tour, working in the Communications Centre.

Eric Hughes, Jim Marsh and *Dave Henderson*, civilians who all worked for HQ90 Group, Signals Command and were the IAL interface for all technical specifications.

Technical Information

The following article was written by the author and appeared in *The Craftsman*, Vol.2, No.3 in August 1960. I hope those readers who are technically inclined will find it of historic interest, especially as 'satellite' data and voice communication was just around the corner.

The *Craftsman* journal was published periodically as the bulletin of HQ Signals Command at Medmenham in the UK, on behalf of its subordinate formations and all telecommunications sections of the Royal Air Force. It was issued to selected RAF formations as well as certain Commonwealth activities.

The *Craftsman* was intended purely as a source and exchange medium for information on telecommunications which could be of value in training and to stimulate discussion and interest in its readers.

The publication was intended for Airmen and Officers alike, whose duties were in the field of communications.

From my point of view it was very satisfying to see that Gan was soon appearing at the top of the traffic league tables that were published in this journal. This fact, I believe, fully justified the considerable effort that went into the design, development and manufacture of the CCS control desk and associated equipment by my employer IAL in conjunction with the RAF. I would like to think that my efforts also made some small contribution to its success. Unless the RAF personnel at Medmenham had not had the foresight to ensure I was posted to Gan then my only contribution to the RAF would probably have been in keeping some of their kitchen utensils clean in a tin room at a mess in the outer reaches of Yorkshire. Thank you RAF.

CCS GAN (by Junior Technician M. Butler)

The CCS at the Communications Centre Gan is the most modern system in use in the Royal Air Force. Furthermore it is entirely new in its conception in so far as the section is completely remote from the Message Centre and control is exercised through the medium of semi-automatic signalling between us and the operating staff. Given personnel who are fully experienced in the art of Circuit Control, a CCS such as ours can, without any doubt, reach greater heights of efficiency than have ever been dreamed of to date.

Unfortunately, all of our staff are entirely new to the **CAF** Network and as a result we are still rather in the dark as to some of the finer points of controlling. However, the day will come no doubt when other stations are fitted with this type of control, or perhaps some reader may even be "fortunate" enough to be posted to Gan and consequently I feel that a general description of the section may not be amiss.

The control system at Gan provides for full duplication of all channels passing through the Circuit Control Section. This facility together with a comprehensive system of channel switching ensures the minimum disruption of traffic during frequency changing. Facilities are also incorporated for the speedy "Patching Out" of faulty equipment and re-allocation of traffic lines to and from the message centre. Circuit state information is provided for CCS, Cipher Room and **DSO** by means of a semi-automatic light indication system.

The section building itself not only houses the CCS but also the Receivers and **VHF** Transmitters for the station. The complete set-up being operated by four men per watch. The section breaks down into six main parts. On the receive side, (1) Receivers, (2) Line Patching Bay, (3) **VF** Equipment, (4) Monitoring teleprinter jackfield, (5) Channel switching console and (6) Channel patching jackfield. The 'send' side is of course, a duplicate of the foregoing, substituting transmitters for receivers.

Facilities for the patching out of faulty equipment in the message centre and the re-routing of send and receive traffic lines are provided. by the "Channel Patching Jackfield". Incorporated in this unit is a milliammeter for checking line currents and a **TDMS** thus, when used as a "Test Calls Generator", it can be patched into any of the traffic lines. Also available on this jackfield. are regenerative repeaters which are normally used for CAF patching. If a live traffic line is broken for any reason, such as a mis-patch at the jackfield, an automatic bell alarm will warn the operator of the fault.

The "Channel Switch Console" forms part of the main CCS control desk. Two such consoles are fitted at Gan, each having eighteen switching strips. Each of these strips is associated with one channel of an **SSB** circuit and has switches for routing traffic on the 'send' and 'receive' side of either duplicated systems, i.e. Red or Yellow. **FSK** circuits can be routed via the desk and if simplex, only require one switching strip.

This strip also incorporates lamps which give visual warning if a predetermined amount of distortion is exceeded on either send or receive side, each side having its own separate lamp.

Two green lamps are fitted to indicate the Security State of the associated channel and this indication is brought up automatically when the security equipment is inserted in the line. Two illuminating push buttons, amber in colour, are fitted, one associated with 'send' and one with 'receive'. If the outgoing traffic is found to be corrupt due, say, to a 5-Unit fault, the appropriate push-button is depressed. This action will give the message centre an audible and visual flashing light-alarm of corrupt traffic. It is then their responsibility to report the fault to 5-Unit workshops or, if necessary, to request us to switch consoles for them.

Notification that the warning has been received in the message centre and that the necessary action is being taken is given by depression of an "**ACK** CCS" button which will extinguish both alarms and the amber light on the CCS desk. On the receive side, if the message centre is receiving corrupt traffic they warn CCS by depression of a "CALL CCS" button associated with the channel in question. This causes the 'push-button' on the receive side of the switching strip to flash and an audible alarm to sound. CCS acknowledge the report by depressing the flashing button which stops all alarms.

It is possible to change the receive system from "RED" to "YELLOW" and vice versa whilst traffic is actually passing, the change being effected by a single key which has three positions, Mark - Traffic Red - Traffic Yellow. Consequently, provided the alternative system is maintained in full radio communication the instantaneous change-over should permit unbroken communication throughout the 24 hours.

On the send side, CCS test calls are fed from a 6S5 auto-head on to a calls "busbar" which is incorporated in the 'switching console' and thus, again by means of a single switch, it is possible to change from "Traffic" to "Calls merely by the flick of a key. Once again this switch has three positions. Mark - Test Calls - Traffic.

The "Monitor Teleprinter Jackfield" enables, us to check any traffic line in or out of the section as to its suitability for traffic. A milliammeter is built in for the checking of line currents. The teleprinters associated with this jackfield have pilot relays to keep line loading down to a minimum. Eight teleprinters are available for checking the circuits, six being receive only and the other two being full send and receive.

VF equipment is the normal Two-Tone Six Channel type and a separate rack is provided for each system.

As receivers and CCS are integral at Gan, no alternative line route is provided. Outgoing 'tones' however, can be patched on a "Line Patching Bay" to either main or alternative **SHF** Transmitters located in the receiver room which provide a 4000 **Mc/s** Radio Link to the transmitters proper at Hithadhoo, 7 miles away.

An extremely comprehensive test and alarm system is built into the desk. On this it is possible to select any tone or **DC** line within the system and to check line levels, distortion and line polarity. The composite tones of any SSB signal can be heard by means of a monitoring amplifier and by further selection of key and rotary switches, the Mark and Space tones of any individual channel can be selected. Built into the test equipment is a test detector and a set of filters which can be used for comparison checks with the normal working VF. This enables swift location of VF faults. The alarm system gives both visual and audible warning in the event of a power failure, fuse rupture, line discontinuity or circuit alarm from the message centre.

Located on the control desk are two teleprinters, one for liaison with transmitters and the other liaison with a distant terminal, the termination being selected by means of key switches situated on a panel adjacent the teleprinter. Lamp calling facilities are also on this panel as well as a Speed Converter Control Button, for use with 45 baud speed circuits. In addition to the liaison on the control desk there are external teleprinters connected to each channel through an 'External Liaison Teleprinter Jackfield' facilitating the patching of printers to the various circuits.

I have not gone into the technical description of the set-up. To do so would be impossible in an article of this nature, however, I hope that my foregoing general look at the section will have proved interesting and provided some insight into the appearance of CCSs of the future. *(Article ends)*

Abbreviations used in the above article

CCS	Communications Control System
CAF Network	Commonwealth Air Force Network
DSO	Duty Signals Office
VHF	Very High Frequency
VF	Voice Frequency
TDMS	Telegraph Distortion Measuring Set
SSB	Single Side Band
FSK	Frequency Shift Keying
ACK	ACKnowledge
SHF	Super High Frequency
Mc/s	Mega cycles per second
DC	Direct Current

RED and YELLOW traffic operation

In the 1960s, in order to ensure uninterrupted data traffic flow, as far as possible, on the SSB and FSK CAF circuits within the RAF, frequency prediction charts were used to set up the most appropriate receiver and transmitter frequencies for any particular time of day and the date. These frequencies were set up on the "RED" system say, and the next predicted frequencies were set up on the "YELLOW" system. When channel traffic conditions indicated a deterioration in the original "RED" selected frequencies then the "YELLOW" system was switched into service. The original "RED" system was then set to the next predicted frequencies for the selected traffic circuits. This alternating between "RED" and "YELLOW" systems improved traffic flow efficiencies considerably and minimised message traffic re-runs.

The only disadvantage, if you can call it that, was that there always had to be a duplicate set of transmitters and receivers for each CAF circuit. That is, one set of equipment for the "RED" system and one for the "YELLOW". This was a small price to pay for the greater efficiency achieved.

Michael Butler

ABBREVIATIONS

RAF	Royal Air Force
RAFA	Royal Air Force Association
HM	Her Majesty's
AOC	Air Officer Commanding
CO	Commanding Officer
MO	Medical Officer
Sq Ldr	Squadron Leader
Flt Lt	Flight Lieutenant
WO	Warrant Officer
NCO	Non Commissioned Officer
J/T	Junior Technician
SAC	Senior Air Craftsman
MP	Military Police
KD	Khaki Drill
UK	United Kingdom
MPs	Members of Parliament
MOD	Ministry Of Defence
AMWD	Air Ministry Works Department
AD	Air Ministry Department
HQ	HeadQuarters
ATC	Air Traffic Control
CCS	Communications Control System
Comms	Communications
MT	Motor Transport
HSL	High Speed Launch
BFPO	British Forces Post Office
PO	Post Office
NAAFI	Navy Army & Air Force Institutes
WVS	Women's Voluntary Service
BBC	British Broadcasting Corporation
ITV	Independent TeleVision
IAL	International Aeradio Limited
AT&E	Associated Telephones & Equipment
NHM	Natural History Museum
MHz	Mega Hertz
U/S	UnServiceable

Tailpiece

After taking some fourteen days leave over the Christmas and New Year period, 1960-1961, I reported for work at RAF Stanbridge near Leighton Buzzard, Buckinghamshire in the UK. Over the Christmas leave period I had purchased a new car. This was one of the frog-eyed Austin Healey Sprites and I used this to travel from my home in Hemel Hempstead to Stanbridge.

I was told that accommodation at RAF Stanbridge for single men was virtually non-existent and would I mind looking for my own digs somewhere locally. I was informed that a living out allowance would be available to help with the cost of renting my own rooms. Since it only took me about twenty minutes to get from my home in Hemel Hempstead to Stanbridge I commuted to work each day. My National Service good fortune continued.

The new IAL manufactured CCS control desk and associated equipment had already been installed by a fitting party from RAF Henlow. These guys really had made an excellent job of the installation and the equipment was in the final stages of commissioning. My services were used to help in this process and the whole system was soon being used to control all the CAF circuits through the centre. I was not asked to go on watch again, for which I was very thankful, and I worked a conventional 0830 to 1700 Hours day from Monday to Friday.

The Officer in charge of the Communications Centre obviously knew of my background and involvement with the Gan equipment and asked if I would be prepared to write some operating instructions relating to all the Comms equipment based on my experience in Gan. This I willingly agreed to do and over a four month period produced operational procedures for each major item of hardware within the CCS.

When not involved with writing about the CCS equipment I was detailed to help the daytime servicing staff with preventative maintenance on other communications equipment within the

Commcen. Some of the Time Division Multiplexing Equipment was quite a challenge since it relied on synchronised motor driven contacts for its operation. Setting up these contacts accurately certainly was a precision job which I enjoyed immensely.

My two years National Service came to an end on 19th July 1961 and I was put on the reserve list for three and a half years. I really counted myself very lucky that I had spent a very useful two years gaining valuable experience in my chosen career and seeing parts of the world that up to then I had only dreamed of.

After a few days' leave I went job hunting and attended a series of interviews with various communications manufacturers. I also visited my old boss at IAL and he offered me a job with excellent prospects and a salary which far exceeded other offers. I therefore rejoined my old company and immediately became involved in the **Master Engineering Control Centre (MECC)** Equipment for the RAF's "Skynet" satellite project. But that is yet *another* story.

Michael Butler. April 2000

RAF Gan 1960. Valiant Bomber.

Return to Gan
1998

1998. Hotel Waterfront (above); Swimming Pool (below).

Return to Gan, 1998

Our Emirates Airlines flight from London Heathrow via Dubai to Male, capital of the Maldives, was singularly uneventful. It was punctuated only by the visits of very attentive and friendly staff with the drinks trolley and to deliver meals on a regular basis. It was the best airline food that Diane and I had tasted for many years. No wonder that they were voted "Airline of the Year" in 1998, an accolade that they thoroughly deserved.

The Boeing 777 aircraft, which we flew in on both legs of our journey to Male, were very comfortable and had the added bonus of a flat screen television mounted in the back of each passenger's seat. One of the channels was connected to a camera mounted close to the nose-wheel of the plane and this provided passengers with an excellent view of pullback, taxiing, take-off and landing. Other channels provided for a variety of up-to-date films to suit all tastes, as well as an on-line map showing the exact aircraft's position, height, speed and time to destination.

We took off from Heathrow, on schedule, at 1345 hours on Friday 2 October for the 8½ hours flight to Dubai and landed there in the early hours of Saturday morning. What an international crossroads Dubai airport is. It appeared to us to be even busier than Heathrow in spite of it being so early. We had just over three hours stopover at Dubai before our scheduled flight to Male was due.

We made the most of this time by visiting the Dubai Duty Free Shopping area. What an Aladdin's cave this is. You name any luxury good and almost without exception, you will find it at Dubai duty free at a very reasonable price. It is the only duty free, that I am aware of, that sells cars. Mercedes, BMW, and a variety of 4 wheel off-road machines are all on offer with delivery to anywhere in the world.

One of the other perks to be had at Dubai duty free is the ability to purchase a raffle ticket for each of two prestige cars. This raffle takes place on a continuous basis and is open to any bonafide arriving, departing or transit traveller. When 1000 tickets have been sold the draw takes place conducted by the Director General, Department of Civil Aviation. The only problem is that tickets cost some £88 each. This is equivalent to Dh500 or US$139. It is not bad odds considering that if you do win a car then you will be flown Business Class to Dubai for the presentation. The prize also includes free shipment of your vehicle back to your country of residence, but they do not pay any import duty that may be due.

The flight from Dubai took about 4 hours and we landed at Hulule International Airport, Male, about 0845 hours on Saturday morning. Landing at Male is just like landing on an aircraft carrier since the airport buildings and runway totally dominate one, very long, island. Male's main commercial and shopping centre and hotels are all on an adjacent island a short boat ride away.

We passed through immigration and customs having completed the required forms prior to landing and then collected our luggage before going through a customs check. We had been told prior to landing that it was strictly forbidden to bring alcohol into the Maldives, an Islamic country. If you did, then it had to be lodged with customs and collected just prior to your return flight home. Alcohol is available to visitors at all holiday resorts within the Republic of the Maldives but if you get caught smuggling it in, then it will be confiscated and your holiday could be terminated before it has begun.

Diane and I soon located the Kuoni holiday representative who informed us that the Air Maldives flight to Gan would be called about 1200 hours. We were taken to a small cafe near the terminal building and asked if we would like a drink. With the temperature on Male about 85°F and a light breeze blowing we decided on a Coca-Cola each. Having drunk these we were then charged $6US for the privilege (about £3.90). The drinks were cold and the "genuine article", however we did think the charge excessive. If this was to be a foretaste of things to come then we were glad we had gone for an all inclusive holiday package.

We checked in for our Air Maldives flight to Gan just after midday and were told that departure time would be 1315 hours. This time came and went and there was still no sign that we were to board the aircraft. We could see the aircraft outside the departure lounge, it was a De Havilland Dash 7 twin turbo prop plane. There was considerable activity around the plane and it was then announced that for technical reasons the aircraft was delayed and the new departure time would be 1430 hours.

By now, both we and the other 30 passengers waiting to board the aircraft, were feeling rather hungry. After another hour we were told that we could go to the airport restaurant where we would be provided with a meal with the compliments of Air Maldives. The meal was delicious, a chicken curry with rice, hurriedly prepared by a very capable chef and his kitchen staff. We had just finished the meal when it was announced that all was well with the aircraft and we were to board immediately.

The Dash 7 was soon at its cruising altitude of 15000 feet and we were looking down on just some of the 1,190 islands that are grouped into the 26 main atolls forming the Republic of the Maldives. From our advantage point it could be seen that many of the islands were uninhabited whilst on others buildings and roads were clearly visible.

After an hours flying time the aircraft descended and landed to drop off some passengers at an island in the Haddunmaht Atoll. We were soon on our way again with the Addoo Atoll only some 20 minutes flying time away.

It was fortunate that we had been allocated seats on the port side of the aircraft as very shortly we were approaching the Gan runway from the Northwest. The plane's approach to Gan was down the outer reef side of Hithadhoo, Hankede, Maradhoo, Maradhoofeydhoo, and Feydhoo. Each island was visible from our window and the new causeways joining the islands could be clearly seen.

We touched down on Gan around 1615 hours. Not being someone who is prone to showing very much emotion, I certainly found a lump in my throat and a nervous expectancy at being back on Gan after leaving nearly 39 years earlier. Not in my wildest dreams did I ever expect to return to this island in the sun. Now I was back and able to share the experience of having a 10-day holiday here with my wife.

The first thing I noticed about Gan, since leaving in December 1960, was the total island explosion in trees, bush, scrub and plants in general. The majority of the island buildings were so swallowed up in the profusion of growth that it was almost impossible to recognise any old familiar landmarks. All, that is, except the aircraft control tower that looked exactly like I remembered it.

We disembarked and made our way to a new terminal building whilst the aircraft was unloaded. Not the convenience here of a motorised vehicle for the passengers luggage. A hand pulled trolley was soon being unloaded and we picked out our cases and took them to the waiting "Ocean Reef Club" bus outside. There is nowhere else to stay in Addoo Atoll. Whilst waiting for our luggage I had been talking to the local Maldivian bus driver and indicated that this was not my first trip to Gan. He spoke excellent English and we were soon talking about old times with the RAF. By this time everyone had collected their baggage and we all boarded the bus. The driver offered Diane and I the two front seats of the bus and we thanked him for his warm welcome.

A few minutes ride and we were turning right into the Ocean Reef Club, going down the narrow driveway through well-manicured gardens and lawns, and pulling up outside the Hotel reception area. Emmanuella met us, an Eastern European lady who spoke many languages fluently and was employed by the hotel to welcome new guests, organise site seeing trips, and generally to look after the guests welfare. We were all provided with a welcoming fruit punch drink and Emmanuella soon outlined all the information relating to our stay in the Hotel in particular and in the Addoo Atoll in general.

We were taken to our room, 102, close to the main hotel complex. Instructions on the use of the Air Conditioning system were given as well as in the operation of the bathroom shower. What luxury! No air-conditioning or room showers in 1960, just a fan suspended from the ceiling and communal showers in the centre of our billet block. We were going to enjoy our stay on Gan especially as our first evening meal was from a barbecue arranged in the gardens and around the swimming pool area.

Neither of us had had any sleep on the journey to Gan, apart from the odd catnap. After a really tasty barbecue meal and drinks at a table under the stars, we now felt replete and very tired, so returned to our room and almost instantly fell asleep.

We awoke Sunday morning, well after sunrise, to hear the wind in the palm trees and the chattering of the "Fairy Terns" amongst the branches. Our room was no more than 10 metres from the waters edge on the lagoon side of the island and the lapping of the waves on the coral sand and against the sea wall could be clearly heard. I had totally forgotten just what a relaxing and peaceful place Gan could be.

The Hotel Complex

The hotel complex has been formed out of the buildings and grounds that were originally part of the RAF's SNCO's Quarters, Mess and the station Sick Quarters. If reference is made to the RAF Gan Grid Layout Plan, Drawing F/034 then buildings referenced 16 to 25 inclusive, 29, 30, and 189, are involved.

The original billets, 16, 17, 18, 22, 23, 24 and 25, have all been modified in the same way to provide rooms for the hotel's guests. The original centralised shower, bath and latrine blocks have all been demolished making each ten-room billet effectively into two 5-room blocks which have then been rejoined in the middle.

Each of the 5 room blocks has been given a face-lift. The original wooden roof and veranda support pillars have been removed and replaced with more substantial circular and shaped concrete ones. Each room now has its own walled, separately lit and covered outside patio area complete with two chairs and a table.

Each room has been modified and now includes a shower, shower curtain, wash hand basin and toilet in a separately walled area. The bathroom area is fully tiled and the shower area floor sunk about an inch to allow for the effective drainage of water. The water for the shower is electrically heated but only cold, or should I say "lukewarm", water is available for the wash hand basin that has a mirror, overhead lighting and a razor socket. The bathroom is not air-conditioned but it has a mosquito meshed and slatted high level window to the outside of the building.

Each bedroom area is well decorated and equipped with a king-size bed as well as a wardrobe, small table and chairs, dressing table and a Mini bar. The large patio sized window looking out on to the gardens is fully curtained. Two bedside tables with drawers and table lamps complete the decoration. All room lighting is controllable from the bedside.

The Air Conditioning units fitted in each room are of the latest type and are controlled by a hand-held controller, very much like a TV controller. One excellent feature of these units is that the main compressor part of the air conditioner, which is the noisiest part, is mounted outside the room, with only the cooling unit and fan actually in the wall of the room itself. With the controller it is very simple to adjust room temperature as well as the humidity level required. You can also program your AC unit to switch on and off at intervals throughout the day should this be required. Setting the air conditioner to a temperature about 2 degrees less than the outside ambient temperature is recommended if headaches, sore throats and chills are to be avoided.

The original SNCO's billet, reference 20, has been demolished and a large fresh water swimming pool has been built in its place. The whole area has been landscaped and non-slip flagstones laid all around the pool area. A bar area has been built in the centre of the pool with barman access to it via a small wooden bridge. Those swimmers using the bar sit on submerged concrete stools. Adjacent to the pool are showers, toilets and a pool maintenance area. The whole area has plenty of sun beds, tables and umbrellas and pool towels are freely available throughout the day. There are also regular visits from the resident barman and from restaurant staff to ensure no one goes thirsty or hungry.

The north-western boundary of the hotel complex has been marked by the building of a substantial concrete wall which extends from the northern shoreline to the wall adjacent to the main road leading to the old RAF Officer's Mess (Building 1). This new wall is virtually parallel to, and just behind buildings 44 and 15, which were Senior Officers and Air Crew Quarters respectively. At the shore end of the wall an additional jetty has been constructed out over the reef and is about as long as the original Officers and NCO's Jetty about 50 metres to the east.

The SNCO's Mess (building 21) remains very much as it was when used by the RAF. Like all other buildings in the hotel complex it has been given a face-lift and now houses the hotels reception area, kitchen and restaurant, lounge, coffee shop and bar areas. The original air conditioned snooker room and table are still intact and there is a table tennis table adjacent to the bar/coffee shop area for the use of the hotels more energetic guests. At one end of the main reception area there is a small gift shop whose tenant specialises in hand painted "T" shirts. The hotel management and administration offices are also housed in the building and a covered area for mountain bikes, for guests' use, completes the main hotel building. Please remember that if you are an ex Ganite from any of the forces, then there is a special visitor's book held in reception that they would like you to sign before leaving.

The SNCO's Tennis Court (19) is still intact but does not appear to have been in use for some time.

The wall just west of the old RAF Gymnasium (290) now forms the hotel complex eastern limit. The RAF (Sick Quarters 29), Mortuary (30), and Medicine Store (189), have all been demolished apart from the hospital's small reception area next to the road. This has been modified and is now the "Eurodivers" shop and dive centre for the Addoo Atoll. Buildings 134 and 292 have also been demolished and the whole area has been set out with gardens, lawns, trees and bushes. The hotel complex is attended to on a daily basis by a team of dedicated gardeners.

VIP's Centre

Those facilities, buildings, grounds, including the shore line, which used to form the RAF Officers and CO's complex are now out of bounds to all visiting Ocean Reef Club guests. These buildings and facilities are used for the accommodation of visiting Maldivian officials. The main access point to this complex is at the end of the Feydhoo/Gan causeway and is usually manned by security guards or secured by locked heavy steel gates. It was not possible to ascertain just how many of the original RAF buildings were still in use. There did not appear to be any noticeable changes.

Eastern Gan Facilities and Buildings

The Corporals and Airmen's club (building 42) is now partly a sports centre and the rest is used to accommodate some shops.

The Swimming Pagar (ref. 10) is disused and in need of major maintenance if ever to be used again. The construction of this pool was completed between August 1967 and August 1968. It was built with flap valves that allowed the sea water to enter and keep it fresh. Soon after it was opened, someone found a Stonefish at the bottom and it was some time before anyone would use it again.

The Airmen's Tennis court (ref. 41) is in use, well maintained, and has floodlighting when required. I assume this is part of the sports centre complex.

The Church (ref. 13) is now a Mosque and is in daily use.

The Guard House (building 11) is still in use and accommodates the security guards looking after access over the Gan/Feydhoo causeway.

Static Water Tank (ref., 12) still exists and had water in it.

Sunday and Monday were the first two full days of our holiday. Emmanuella had organised a snorkelling trip and lunchtime barbecue on the island of Viligili for Monday. Eight other hotel guests and ourselves put our names down to go. We both felt that to spend virtually a whole day in the sun swimming and snorkelling may result in serious sunburn, so Sunday we spent taking it easy around the pool trying to obtain a quick tan.

One of the limitations of travelling on a package tour by air is that the weight of luggage that you are allowed as a tourist class passenger is limited to 20 kilos each. This was the limitation with Emirates Airlines. Like most operators you would have to be seriously over the limit before they levy an excess charge. Air Maldives however impose a limit of 15 kilos per passenger for the Male to Gan leg of the journey because of the limited size of the aircraft and this must be kept in mind when packing cases in the UK. It was also quite suprising to be asked at the check-in for the Air Maldives flight, after checking in our luggage, to be asked to get on the scales ourselves with our hand baggage. We found out later that the main reason for weighing luggage and passengers was not only to ensure that the aircraft was not being overloaded, but also to make sure that the maximum amount of additional freight could be put on the aircraft. All fresh vegetables have to be flown into the Addoo Atoll from Male. If the Air Maldives flight is fully loaded with passengers and luggage then these and other essential goods do not get delivered.

Because of these weight restrictions I had decided to leave my snorkelling flippers (Swimming Fins) in the UK and hire a pair on Gan. As Diane's snorkelling and swimming experience was limited she had decided to bring along a buoyancy jacket, borrowed from a friend who has a canoe. This did nothing to help keep the weight of our baggage down. We had also brought with us our snorkelling masks. My mask was the same one that I used on virtually a daily basis during my time on Gan with the RAF. It is still fully serviceable and has been used on many overseas holidays since that time.

The Diving School at the Ocean Reef is run by Eurodivers whose instructors speak English, German, and Italian. PADI Open Water and Assistant Instructor courses are available as well as a whole range of organised dives around the Addoo Atoll for certificated Scuba divers. Eurodivers were more than happy to hire me a pair of Swimming Fins for a charge of $1US per day, and would have been able to provide Diane with a buoyancy aid had she not brought one with her.

We met the Eurodivers Manager, Mr Karel Ververgaart, on a number of occasions as he was also resident at the hotel. He told us that one of the best Scuba dives in the Atoll was on the wreck of the ship "British Loyalty".

It was in 1944 that this British Merchant Ship was anchored inside the lagoon near Viligili. This was considered a safe anchorage as all the main channels into the lagoon had been fitted with antisubmarine nets. Some seven days before the attack took place on this boat the whole base had been put on alert after a high-flying aircraft had been spotted. Aircraft from the base took off but they found no sign of the plane. Just a week later a Japanese submarine managed to find a hole through the Gan Channel net and fired a torpedo diagonally at the ship. This attack took place at night and the subsequent explosion wakened the entire population on the Atoll. The following morning a large oil slick was visible but the ship was still afloat. Luckily no one was killed in the attack but the ship was so badly damaged that it remained where it had been anchored. The British forces cleaned up the oil slick and it was not until after the war ended that the British Loyalty was towed to just south-east of Hithadhoo and scuttled.

The ship, which is some 140 metres long with a beam of 20 metres, now lies on the bottom on its starboard side in about 33 metres of water and is heavily encrusted with both hard and soft corals. Many fish have made their homes in these corals and large turtles swim around the deck. According to Karel this is one of the most spectacular dives in the lagoon and a *must* for visiting Scuba divers. For those with access to Admiralty Chart 2067 the wrecks position is at :

Longitude 73 degrees 07 minutes East of Greenwich

Latitude 0 degrees 38 minutes and 4 seconds South.

On Monday, as instructed by Emmanuella, we all gathered in the reception area of the hotel at 0930 hours for the Viligili trip. Emmanuella led us the three-minute walk to the main Gan Jetty where we boarded the boat. A few drops of rain began to fall and we were glad that the seating area of the boat was fully covered. The rain did not last long and we were soon in glorious sunshine again, tempered by a fairly strong south-easterly breeze. Emmanuella did not accompany us on this occasion but the three crew were joined by one of the hotel waiters who was in charge of the food, drinks and barbecue.

As we made our way to the reef at the northern end of Viligili we passed a large Texaco oil tanker which had come into the lagoon overnight. We later learnt that the ship had developed a major leak due to cracked stern plates and had anchored so that repairs could be carried out. Luckily it was not carrying any oil and any pollution threat was minimal.

During our 35 minute ride to the reef we were all amused to see the older member of the ships crew assemble a collection of plastic drainpipes on the deck and down into the depths of the boat below. A piece of cloth was secured to a pole and this was thrust down one of the drainpipes. This contraption turned out to be one of the most effective bilge pumps I have ever seen. It was a little worrying to see the amount of water that was being removed as the crewmember continuously pumped throughout the journey.

We were soon anchored up in some 20 feet of water above the reef and everyone donned mask and flippers. A rusting ladder was put over the side and in we all went. As was expected there were many dozens of different varieties of fish but I was disappointed to see that some 90 to 95% of the coral reef was dead. Diane soon gained confidence in the buoyancy aid she was wearing and we swam out into deeper water over the reef edge. Although we could see some living clumps of coral at these greater depths it was by no means in the profusion that I remembered back in the 1960's.

We swam into shallower water and I made my initial attempt at taking underwater pictures of some of the more brightly coloured fish with the underwater Minolta camera I had purchased for that very purpose. The camera had auto focus, a built in flash and was suitable to be used down to depths of 10 metres. The thing I found most awkward was trying to look through the viewfinder whilst wearing a facemask. In the end I resorted to holding the camera at arms length and working on the basis of "point and shoot". As I found out later shots taken within 6 feet of the sea surface with the flash on were ok and the colours of the fish were well reproduced. However, shots deeper than 6 feet tended to be very blue as the water filtered out the natural colours of the fish and surroundings, even if the flash was used.

After some 1½ hours of snorkelling we all returned to the boat. The anchor was raised and the captain made his way down the coast of Viligili on the lagoon side of the island.

After some very careful navigation and with the help of his crew the boat was steered in over the reef and anchored just off the beach where the island is at its narrowest point. The water here is very shallow and the coral heads have to be avoided if damage to the hull is not to occur. Viligili is uninhabited and we were soon all on shore doing our "Robinson Crusoe" act exploring the flora and fauna. Two minutes walk and you were on the sea reef side of the island with the waves pounding down on the outer reef no more than 20 metres away.

One of the crew was soon climbing up a coconut tree and removing young coconuts. He threw these down and the waiter cut into the tops of these and offered everyone a drink. Everyone agreed the drink to be very refreshing and the young coconut inside was white, jelly like and very tender.

The captain and crew were soon dispatched to gather wood for the fire whilst the hotel waiter constructed the stand for the cooking utensils and barbecue proper. Soon smoke was lazily drifting through the coconut palms as fresh fish started to cook. Rice was put on to boil as ice cold drinks were distributed to all. What a great way to spend a day. It was just a little surprising to see a large linen tablecloth spread on the ground with palm tree logs spread around it to act as seats. We were all invited to eat and as you can imagine the fish tasted just great. Fresh fruit was our dessert.

When everyone had eaten there fill, and plates, serviettes and litter cleared away, the waiter and crew had their lunch. Some of our party lay on the beach, some swam in the shallows and some continued their exploration of the island.

The elder member of the crew had soon completed eating and showed those of us on the beach just how the local palm branches could be woven to produce baskets, trays and even waterproof panels for use in constructing traditional Maldivian Houses. Even though he may have been the oldest member of the crew is was he who had shinned up the tree and cut down the coconuts. It was great to know these traditional skills have not been lost in spite of more modern methods being employed now for local house building. Other members of the crew now arrived and amused us all by organising Hermit Crab races along the palm logs.

All too soon it was time to leave but the captain agreed to anchor up again on the reef edge for another half-hours snorkelling. About five of the party went back into the water again but both Diane's and my shoulders were telling us that this would be unwise. We were soon motoring back to the Gan jetty, taking in the beautiful views and reflecting on the really great time we had had that day.

Industry on Gan

Soon after arriving on Gan we had become aware of the existence of two new factory complexes. These were both clothing factories and were operated on a 24-hour per day basis. One was operated by "Linear Clothing (Maldives) Pty Ltd" and the other by "Eden Fashions (Maldives) Pty Ltd." We were told, but had no means of checking, that "Linear Clothing" was associated with the "Ralph

Lauren" Fashion Empire and "Eden Fashions" with the "House of Fraser" group.

The workers who manned the machines in both factories are ladies from Sri Lanka.

They are flown into the Maldives by the companies on the basis of a yearly contract. After a year they are able to return home, terminate their employment or renew their contract for a further year if they wish to.

We were informed that the main reason that these two factories were set up on Gan was because Sri Lanka had got to the point of fully meeting its allowable export quotas as far as clothing was concerned. The only way it would be allowed to export further textiles was if the factories were built outside the country. Since unemployment is still very high in Sri Lanka it became economical to fly the Sri Lanka workforce out to Gan. A considerable amount of American investment has been made in these two factories with the controlling companies benefiting from a relatively cheap labour force.

There appears to be a considerable amount of resentment by the local Maldivian population at the influx of this foreign workforce. This is especially so as only a few local Maldivians are employed in the factories. It was suggested to us that another reason could be because of the relatively low wages that were offered.

The Sri Lankan lady workforce all live on Gan and are housed in the original Airmen's Billets at the north-eastern side of the island. These billets are secured by a high steel mesh fence that totally encloses the accommodation. Additional Billet type accommodation has been built within the compound. It was possible to observe that in my old Billet, number 47, room 8, there were now a total of 5 double bunks. We used to think that with 6 guys per billet it was getting a little crowded. With 10 ladies per room it must, at times, be pretty uncomfortable especially as there is no air conditioning and only a central room fan.

As far as could be ascertained from outside of the accommodation compound the following Airmen's Billets are still in use for the factory workforces. Billet numbers 37, 47, 48, 49, 51, 52, 53, 58, 59, and 60. There appeared to be one new single accommodation block built alongside billets 37, and 52 and a two-storey accommodation block next to billet 47 and the compound access gates.

The Airmen's Mess is still being used in its original role and now caters for the factory workforces.

The "Linear Clothing" factory had been built alongside the road just to the east of the old Astra Cinema (ref. 120), whilst the "Eden Fashions" factory had been built on the site of the NAAFI Bulk Stores (ref. 103 and 104), on the opposite side of the road. We were informed by guests at the Hotel that conducted tours around the factories were on offer and when they had visited they were invited to stay and have lunch with the management and workforce.

It was Tuesday 6th October and Diane and I had decided to take a bike ride around Gan. We collected a couple of mountain bikes from the hotel, made sure the brakes were ok and started off in a counter clockwise direction around the island. The sun was shining brightly but there was a strong breeze blowing. We were soon passing by my old billet and waving to the security man controlling traffic across the runway.

I stopped to do some camcorder filming on the centre line of the runway and soon noticed that all the approach lighting which had been on metal gantries out on the reef had now gone, that is, except for one or two rusting steel pillars protruding just above the sea. All the other main runway lighting appeared to be intact and this was confirmed when we saw a night landing later on in our holiday.

We continued our ride, passing the Transformer Distribution Centres and Standby Set House (ref. 201, 202, 203). The Standby Set House did not appear to be in use and we were soon approaching the site of the old Pakistani Camp. Virtually the whole camp has been raised to the ground save the Maldivians' Friday Mosque and one or two minor buildings on the reef side of the road. The reclaimed land has been planted with banana palms and bread fruit trees. There is a large stone plaque on the side of the road recording the fact that this was the site of the Pakistani encampment.

One other item that had escaped demolition was a steel water tower and tank. We thought this was now used to supply the Mosque with water as well as a security hut just down the road.

Continuing our journey we soon came across an abandoned bus at the side of the road. Its engine had been removed and there was no glass in the windows. It appeared that it had been left where it had terminally expired and was now used by plantation workers to shelter from the sun or rain when necessary.

The coral road continued through a tunnel of overhanging branches. The vegetation was so thick that it was impossible to see the reef or sea some 20 metres to our right. We reached a fork in the road and discovered that the right hand fork went out on to a road that had been built out across the southern sea reef. This road had been used for transporting coral, blasted from the reef, back onto Gan for use in building projects. We were amazed to see that even this narrow strip of coral now had many trees and bushes growing on its banks. Unfortunately, as we soon discovered, it was now being used as the island's rubbish dump. The smell was awful and there were hundreds of flies around as well as mosquitoes. We had hoped to go out on this spit of land to take a closer look at the outer reef edge but neither of us really fancied cycling past this partially burning and very smelly tip.

Our journey continued eastwards along the coast line road and I began to look for the CCS/Receiver station where I had been gainfully employed for a year during my National Service with the RAF. The first, and only, thing I did recognise as we emerged from our foliage tunnel into a small clearing was the Static water tank which had featured so prominently in our leaving party in December 1960. It appeared that all the original RAF buildings had been demolished and standing on this site was now a tall Surveillance Radar building. We cycled up the small approach path and very soon an engineer appeared having been alerted to our presence by the local Maldivian cleaning inside the building's entrance. Unfortunately the engineer spoke very little English and after confirming that it was a Radar Station he waved us on our way. I do not think he understood how I had managed to work on this site all those years ago.

Just opposite the Radar Station we found a gap in the trees and bushes which led to the shoreline and from here we managed to get a good view of the rubbish tip road to our right and a view out over the reef. It was at this point out on the edge of the reef that a bulldozer had become stuck whilst in the process of clearing some of 11,000 palm trees from Gan in 1959 to make way for the new staging post. Yes, parts of the bulldozer were still there out on the reef. It was no longer recognisable as a bulldozer, only as different size lumps of rusting metal spread over many metres. I intended to return to the reef at low tide to try and obtain some closer pictures but did not get around to it.

As we continued cycling along we noticed a number of derelict buildings on our left-hand side. I believe that these were originally the Pyrotechnic, Dangerous Goods, Detonator and Explosive Stores, (refs. 271, 272, 273 and 313). Just a short distance further on we looked for signs of the Police Dog Training Centre (ref. 311), but we could find no trace of it.

We cycled on and were looking for the old rifle range and store (ref. 334), but the whole area was so overgrown that nothing was visible. We did however find the old walled cemeteries. Before leaving the UK I had been asked by the Archivist of the RAF Changi Association if I could try and identify just who was buried in these grounds. Unfortunately due to the growth of plants, trees and bushes it was impossible to get into one of the walled areas where at least two gravestones could be seen in the thick undergrowth. We did eventually find a way into the second cemetery and found just one identifiable grave. This was marked to "**Ted Easley 1928 – 1995**". Further enquiries suggested that Ted had spent most of his life in the Maldives and a considerable amount of time in the Addoo Atoll, and, as he had no known living relatives, his dying wish was to be buried on Gan. No one seemed to know what he had been doing during his time in the Maldives. He must have one of the most peaceful graves anywhere in the world.

It was now approaching midday, we were both very hot, feeling hungry and the mosquitoes were biting badly. We therefore agreed to return to the hotel, have some lunch and spend the rest of the day relaxing on the beach or around the pool.

We cycled past the runway security post at the Gan Channel end of the island and made our way back to the Ocean Reef Club. On our way back we passed the old aviation fuel tanks, the Power station, the Airport terminal buildings, the two new clothing factories, the Astra Cinema, the old Station HQ buildings and the main Gan Jetty. We resolved to explore these landmarks another day.

Emmanuella had been busy again and for Wednesday morning had organised another snorkelling trip, this time to Bushy Island. This uninhabited island is on the northern side of the Addoo Atoll and is situated between the Kuda and Maa sea channels. It is the only island in the Addoo Atoll to have a shipping navigation light. It flashes on for 2 seconds every 10 seconds and, with good visibility, can be seen at least 7 nautical miles away. Considering the amount of submerged reef on the northern side of the Atoll this light must be a very welcome sight for any sailor attempting to navigate these waters at night. What I could not find out and would really like to know is, just how these types of lights are powered? It is certainly not connected to the mains electrical power available on the major inhabited islands in Addoo.

This snorkelling trip was a relatively short one and we expected to be back at the hotel by 1300 hours. Emmanuella joined us on this occasion, ostensibly to look after two young members of a Swiss family, also staying at the Ocean Reef. We travelled to Bushy on the same boat as we had for the Viligili trip with the same crew. The drainpipe bilge pump worked fine all the way and we were soon anchored up on the reef just north of the navigational beacon and west of the Maa channel.

We snorkelled for about 1¾ hours and saw large numbers of Surgeon, Angel, Emperor, Parrot and Trigger fish as well as Bannerfish, Blue Stripped Snapper and many other wonderfully coloured fish species. I continued to snap with the underwater camera. At least two of the party saw a small Grey Reef Shark, but we were not that lucky. I suspect panic may have set in with my better half if we had seen it. Once again the majority of the coral on the reef was dead with only a few areas showing signs of life. On another trip to Bushy later on in the week the party of snorkellers were lucky enough to see Dolphins as well as a large number of Turtles. Unfortunately we were not on that trip.

We returned to Gan and after an excellent midday meal followed by forty winks on a lounger by the poolside we decided to walk up the main road to the jetty and explore around this area.

We approached the old European NAAFI shop (ref. 69), opposite the end of the main jetty, only to discover that the building now housed at least two small coffee/snack shops with tables outside under the trees. We received a cheery "hello" from a local gentleman sitting at one of the tables who, it turned out, owned one of the shops. His name was Mohammed and as soon as he knew I was ex RAF he told us to wait, scuttled back into his shop and emerged with a photo album and other pieces of paper.

Mohammed had been a waiter in the RAF Officers' Mess and had been chosen to serve at table when Princess Alexander and other members of the royal family had visited Gan during the 1970's. He had copies of many photographs taken during the visit as well as an original menu and internal RAF memos relating to the organisation required for the meal. He was obviously extremely proud of his association with the RAF and of his participation in this royal visit.

We both thanked him very much for sharing his memories with us and for showing us the photographs. I am certain that Mohammed would welcome contact from any ex RAF personnel who return to Gan.

The Gan Jetty

This has changed little in its 40 years of life and it still has all the original mooring stanchions in place. It does however show signs of its age just above the water line. Here the concrete has crumbled away and many of the steel reinforcing rods and girders are exposed and beginning to rust, especially at the reef end of the structure. One noticeable addition to the jetty is the erection of lighting standards down the right-hand side.

The old MCU Slipway (ref. 117) is still in use as is the MCU Servicing and Boatwright Building (ref. 118). As another Ex-Ganite found during his holiday to Gan in 1996 the internal steel lattice structure of this high building is rusting away quite badly and I was surprised to see it still standing. One thing that has happened since this visit is that the bottom two rows of corrugated iron sheeting **all** around the structure have been removed. I can only imagine that these sheets have been used elsewhere on a newer and more important building project.

The other significant change to occur since the 1996 visit is to the Maldivian jetty which was built just to the east of the main jetty. As pictures, taken at that time, clearly show this structure was built out on the reef and then swept to the left to form a sheltered harbour for the local boats. The left-hand sweep of this structure, some 50% of the total, has now collapsed into the sea and only a few steel-reinforcing rods can be seen above the surface. I could not find out if this had happened slowly, over the last two years, or that the damage caused was the result of a storm.

The RAF Gymnasium (ref. 290), adjacent to the jetty, is now used as a store. When we visited it, it was stacked with many hundreds of bags of cement as well as bags of granite chippings. Associated buildings 336 and 181 still appeared intact and in use.

Thursday dawned with overcast skies and rain had fallen heavily during the night. Diane and I were a little disappointed at the weather as we had made arrangements through reception to hire a

Taxi for the day to take us to Koattey on Hithadhoo. Koattey is right at the most northerly end of Hithadhoo and the limit of the road system. We had asked if we could have a driver who could speak English and who would be willing to stop when required for us to take pictures. The estimated cost for this was about £30. We thought this very reasonable for a day's hire of an air-conditioned taxi.

The taxi arrived outside reception bang on time at 0930 hours and we set off. Our driver came from Maradhoofeydhoo and we were soon bombarding him with questions as we travelled over the causeway and on to Feydhoo. It soon became fairly obvious from our driver's replies that his command of English was a little limited., so we had to simplify the way we asked the questions. It was still raining but slowly beginning to brighten up. We travelled slowly along the new coral coast road that had been built around the eastern side of Feydhoo. Our driver did his best to avoid the rain filled holes in the road and the chickens that roamed free and seemed to have a death wish. Very young children were also seen, waving or just curious when hearing the car approaching.

We were soon leaving Feydhoo and travelling over the causeway. Here workmen were busy modifying the structure in order to put large steel pipes from the sea to lagoon sides. All the original causeways were built with a totally solid construction and it was found that as the tides changed that there could be up to a metres difference in sea height from one side of the causeway to the other. Environmentalists also suggested that this lack of sea flow from sea to lagoon sides of the islands could be contributing to the decline of the lagoon coral reefs. This situation is now being rectified and all causeways will be modified to allow for the required flow of water.

We had soon travelled through Maradhoofeydhoo, Maradhoo, and the small wooded island of Hankede. We arrived on Hithadhoo and I asked our driver if he could slow so I could see if anything was left of the RAF Transmitting Station at which I had worked on a number of occasions. This area of Hithadhoo has changed considerably and there is now a very wide road cut through the coconut palms from the causeway to Hankede. I soon noticed the concrete mooring pier out on the reef where we had alighted from the RAF Pinnace on many occasions. The long rickety walkway from this pier to the shore had all gone apart from a concrete block on the shoreline.

Driving on slowly we came to a clearing where the old RAF transmitting station had once stood. There was absolutely nothing left. Even the buildings foundations appeared to have been removed. I got out of the car and walked around. The only items I found were what appeared to be two of the large concrete blocks, complete with steel eyes that had been used to secure the 250-foot beacon mast guys. There was nothing else.

Further up the road we came to an earth Satellite station with a very large dish antenna. We were told that this was all part of the Addoo Atolls telephone system. We had been impressed to see that on Gan there were now a number of public telephone boxes and these could be used for International Subscriber Trunk Dialling. We had purchased a phone card and managed at the first attempt to connect to our son in the UK for a brief call. The speech delay was a bit off-putting but signals were crystal clear.

We were soon well into Hithadhoo and passing some newly constructed local administration offices which were not yet occupied. Further on we came to Hithadhoo's Southern Secondary School which was opened in 1993 and was the first school of its type to open outside Male. Pupils from all the islands arrive each day either by school bus or, if they live locally, then by bicycle. Many of which were parked outside the school. The school building is of modern construction and has blue roof tiles. It was obviously well maintained and we were told two of the teaching staff were from the UK.

Throughout our journey we had passed a number of Mosques, houses and some shops. We had now arrived at a boatyard and here a wooden Tuna fishing boat was under construction. We were told that some of the harder woods are shipped in from Sri Lanka, but locally grown timber is also used. It was good to see that the traditional methods of boat building were still being employed with major joints being doweled and not screwed.

Our continuing journey took us past another new factory building and complex that was not yet in use. Our driver did not know what it would finally be used for but thought it may be to do with the fishing industry.

Another boatyard appeared on our left as we approached the top end of Hithadhoo. We stopped again and this time we saw under construction what our driver termed a "Safari" boat. This boat was some 60 feet in length and had a very wide beam. We were told it would be used to take tourists on sight seeing trips around the Atolls and islands as well as on fishing expeditions.

We now turned right and found ourselves on a very narrow road through a thickly wooded area of the island. There were one or two houses spotted amongst the trees but these soon stopped and we found ourselves going along the edge of a large freshwater lake. There were many birds here including Herons and Black Bitterns and it was, we were told, also a gathering place for migrating birds.

As the road went further into the wooded area the overhanging branches almost stopped any further progress and our driver had to get out of the car and remove his car phone aerial to stop it being broken off. We asked him when he had been in this area last and he said about 3 years ago. We made steady if slow progress and eventually stopped just short of Demon Point at Koattey.

Two very strong sea currents meet off this point and this has the effect of causing a large bank of coral debris to build along the northern shoreline. It looks as if a giant excavator had dropped the coral to form a very long and high bank but there is nothing man made about it.

We returned to the car and started the return journey.

Soon the taxi driver was showing us the new regional hospital on Hithadhoo. This was not large by European standards but the 22 beds are more than adequate to meet the needs of the local population. Just outside the hospital was a Pharmacy for the supply of prescribed drugs. The Republic of the Maldives provides free health care for all Maldivians. National Health Service please note!

In the centre of Hithadhoo Diane saw that a number of locals had gathered at the roadside and were purchasing fresh Tuna from a local fisherman. She just had to go and see what was happening, and was soon in conversation with the ladies about their purchases. With permission she took some photographs, thanked them all and we continued on our way.

A little further down the main road we noted a pharmacy and since our son is now in his final year of a Pharmacy degree course at Brighton we stopped to see if the owner would mind if we took some photographs. What a reception we had. Not only was the Pharmacist in the shop but also the local Doctor as well as the pharmacy assistant. The doctor, Dr N Gunasekaran from India, worked at the Abuharee Medical Centre on Hithadhoo, and gave us a rundown of his work in the Maldives and his previous work in India. I managed to capture this with the camcorder. The Pharmacist was very interested in Diane's camera and wished to know just how much such a camera would cost, as he was interesting in purchasing a new one. He was also interested in our son's progress on his pharmacy course.

We took photographs inside the pharmacy and of our newly acquired friends, exchanged addresses, and thanked them all for their hospitality. We promised to send them copies of the pictures we had taken and have since done so.

Our taxi arrived back at the Southern Secondary School just as the pupils were coming out at the end of their scholastic day. Diane was on the opposite side of the road taking photographs out to sea of a coral dredging operation when she found herself surrounded by boys from the school. They were all immaculately turned out in their school uniform even though they were just about to return home. They were all very polite and when asked what their favourite subject was, they said "English". There must be potential material here for the Maldivian diplomatic service. They also wished to have their pictures taken and when I walked over with the camcorder they all gave a cheery wave and giggled self-consciously. The girls however were far more reticent at getting involved with the 'tourists' and stood waiting patiently for the school bus.

Both Diane and I thoroughly enjoyed our encounter with these happy and well adjusted children and their conduct said much about the standard of teaching and discipline in the Maldivian schools.

We stopped on Hankede on our return leg to take more pictures of the now sun drenched beaches and the breakers at the edge of the reef. This was real picture post card material and we made the most of our time. We also took pictures on Feydhoo of house brick manufacturing as well as the work going on at the causeways.

We arrived back at our hotel in the afternoon about 1630 hours . What an interesting day this had turned out to be.

Northern Gan

Five days of our holiday had now gone and we were feeling very relaxed and getting a reasonable protective tan. We decided that on Friday we would borrow the bikes again and return to the Gan Channel end of the island, then slowly make our way back to the hotel and see what buildings were still recognisable on the way

At the eastern end of Gan all the following buildings have been demolished:

291	POL Shelter
295	PSD East F/Trailer Shed
543	PSD Office & DOE Store
547	RAOB
550	Rifle Range indoor
551	Skittle Alley (double Lanes)
552	ATC Storage
554	Police Flt. Accommodation Annex
555	RAFA Club
557	RAF Police Qtrs.

The bare shell of the old ILS building is still standing.

The distribution transformer is no longer in use, but the disused well and building are still in place.

Static water tank has been demolished.

The whole area where these buildings used to stand is now seriously overgrown and it was not possible to get through the undergrowth to the lagoon shoreline.

PSD Fuel Storage Tanks.

Of the eight original large storage tanks only four, (2, 3, 4 & 8) are now still standing and definitely not in use. The two smaller capacity tanks (5 & 6) with the same reference have been demolished.

The storage tanks are still in use and used to store the diesel fuel used for running the Power Station Generators. The Diesel Transfer Pump House is still in use and used to pump fuel into the storage tanks from a Road Oil Tanker. The Tanker picks the fuel up from freighters moored at the main Gan Jetty.

The following associated buildings and facilities for the fuel storage complex are now all derelict.

341   PSD Pump House.
223   Avpin Storage.
293   PSD Officer's/Crew Room.
340   PSD Fire Pump Fresh Water Tank.
342   PSD Offices Toilet Block.
417   PSD Fire PumpHouse.
294   Security Building.
172   PSD Fuel Pump House. EXP
179   PSD Samples Store (no roof).

The Bulk Aviation Fuel Pipe Line (ref. 114), which was used to carry fuel from the Oil Jetty (ref. 81) to the storage tanks has been disconnected at the shoreline end of the oil jetty. How much of this pipeline has been removed on land could not be ascertained due to the dense undergrowth along its old route. The pipes on the Oil Jetty are seriously corroded and a large number of holes can be seen in these aged pipes. A new additional 6-inch pipe has been fitted along the jetty, is well maintained, and is used to supply fuel to a new set of much smaller storage tanks just behind the "Eden Fashions" factory.

The Gan Power Station

Diane and I had reached the Power Station and were idly leaning on our bikes staring through the door at the whirring machinery inside. In all the time I had spent on Gan with the RAF I had never been inside the building and it was, I seem to remember, out of bounds anyway. Suddenly a Pakistani gentleman emerged from the gloomy interior and asked if we would like to look around. What an opportunity and "yes", we could film and take as many pictures as we liked.

Our Pakistani Engineer host told us that the Gan Power Station was due to close in the year 2000 and that Gan's electrical supply would come from a new three set station to be constructed on Hithadhoo at Arif. The supplier of the new station would be Mitsubishi.

At present each island has its own set of generators to supply local needs. Both the clothing factories on Gan have their own power supply generators and will only connect to the Gan Power Station in an emergency. They apparently find "Gan" electrical power far too expensive.

The new Hithadhoo power station will supply all the major inhabited islands in the Atoll with electrical power via a 11kilovolt distribution network connected to locally sited transformer stations for step down to the 230v ac required for consumer use. At present the Gan system works with a 3,300 volt distribution system, so all the existing transformer sites will require major modification.

The Gan Power Station has now been running continuously since 1956, when first installed by the RAF and spares for the diesel engines and generators can no longer be obtained from the original manufacturers. Any necessary spares have to be fabricated in Sri Lanka at considerable cost. I think it says a good deal about the British designed and manufactured diesel electric sets when at least five of the original eight sets are still in working order. It also says a great deal about the dedicated team of engineers and mechanics who have maintained and serviced this equipment for well over 40 years.

We also learnt from the Engineer that the Undersea Cable between Gan and Hithadhoo which was used to supply power to the RAF transmitting Station was no longer intact and had been disconnected at both ends. This cable had been fouled on many occasions by the anchors of boats mooring off Hithadhoo. In order to release the boats, the cable had been cut through on a number of occasions and the ends dropped back in the sea. It had become uneconomical to make repairs so local generators were used to supply the mains power instead.

After our tour we were asked if we could sign the visitor's book and we gladly agreed to do this. We ascended the wooden steps to the switch room and here met the Chief Power Station Engineer. He had been employed by the RAF in 1956 and was now in charge of the station – quite some record.

As we left the building a few simple questions came to mind:
- *Did UK manufacturers bid to supply the new power station and distribution system?*
- *If not why not?*
- *Our local track record in this area was second to none!*
- *Will the new power station still be working as well as the old one in 40+ year's time?*

We continued our bike ride westwards and passed the new airport terminal building. On the opposite side of the road we noted customs administration offices as well as a security building. It was noted that the six lighting towers (ref. 275 – 280 inclusive) for illuminating the aircraft hardstanding (Pan), were still intact. We did not ascertain whether they worked or not.

There is such a profusion of new, modified, and old buildings in this central section of Gan that we gave up trying to identify them. It was made even more difficult by the fact that on quite a few, the reference number originally put there during construction had been removed and on some the number had obviously been changed.

We could not however fail to see the Astra Cinema (120). Immediately 'Tom and Jerry' films sprang to mind with the usual chorus from the audience of "Good old Fred!" (Quimby) at the end of each cartoon. What a coarse lot we were! The Astra is still basically a cinema but is not used on a regular basis. The last time it was used for any period of time was to show the World Football Cup games from France. A receiving satellite dish has been erected outside and feeds new projection equipment inside. I assume that it is also possible to show normal films as well.

We passed the new factory complexes and were soon standing looking from the road at the old Station HQ building, with the Memorial Garden to our left and the Static Water Tank to our right. The circular garden in front of HQ was intact and well cared for, with the flagpole in its centre now carrying the Maldivian Flag. The HQ building is used to house local Gan administration offices. These are not unlike the UKs local council offices. I decided that I would like to look at, and film the Memorial Garden, so Diane left me to it and disappeared around the back of Station HQ, or should I say 'Local Administration Offices'. Sorry, old habits die-hard!

The central and largest stone memorial in this garden was erected after the Second World War and commemorates those who died between 1939 – 1945. The inscription reads:

THOSE COMMEMORATED HERE
DIED IN THE SERVICE
OF THEIR COUNTRY
THE MORTAL REMAINS OF SOME
WERE COMMITTED TO FIRE
AND OTHERS LIE BURIED
ELSEWHERE ON ADDU ATOLL

Another commemorative stone in the garden is inscribed:

ROYAL AIR FORCE GAN
1956 - 1976

The small plaque is topped by a cast concrete crown and is the only recorded evidence in the Addoo Atoll that the RAF were on Gan for 20 years.

In the 1970's two guns that had lain rusting on a Gan shoreline were retrieved, cleaned and installed in the garden. The two inscriptions read:

THIS GUN FORMED PART OF THE DEFENCES OF ADDU
ATOLL IN WWII AT CHRISTMAS 1971 IT WAS RECOVERED
FROM THE SOUTH EAST SHORE OF GAN BY PERSONNEL OF
NUMBER 1125 MARINE CRAFT UNIT WHO REMOVED FROM
IT MANY YEARS ACCUMULATION OF RUST. IT WAS
MOUNTED IN ITS PRESENT POSITION IN MAY 1972

And on the second gun:

THIS GUN FORMED PART OF THE DEFENCES OF ADDU
ATOLL IN WWII AT CHRISTMAS 1971 IT WAS RECOVERED
FROM THE SOUTH EAST SHORE OF GAN BY PERSONNEL OF
THE DEPARTMENT OF THE ENVIRONMENT WHO REMOVED
FROM IT MANY YEARS ACCUMULATION OF RUST. IT WAS
MOUNTED IN ITS PRESENT POSITION IN MAY 1972.

Diane had returned to the garden to find me and said she had found someone whom I should meet. Intrigued we walked behind station HQ where I was introduced to a local Maldivian whose name was Abdullah Massii. He lived on Maradhoofeydhoo with his wife and had been a room boy in the 1960s. He told us that he used to work in the Airmen's Billet number 58 and did so until the RAF left in 1976. He recalled many happy memories of his times looking after the lads and was so sorry when the RAF pulled out. Although he was now working on Gan as a Carpenter at the Mechanical Workshop just South of building 110, he said he was not enjoying his present time as much as when the RAF were on the island.

We discovered that Abdullah had nine children, three boys and six girls. His eldest boy was now the Headmaster of the Primary School on Maradhoo and some of his other children had gone to Male to work. He wished to know if we had a family and what they were doing? It was great to talk to someone who had worked on Gan when I was stationed there. Abdullah had just finished work for the day and just about to cycle home when he and Diane met. We saw Abdullah on one other occasion during our holiday and had another long chat. Since returning to the UK we have written to him and sent him some photographs.

Whilst talking to Abdullah we noticed that building 122, the Sailing Club and Bar has been demolished. However, building 159, the Angling Club Store Boat Shed and the two storey Yacht Club House (177) are still standing. The former is now a small restaurant and the latter partly used as a store for the restaurant.

Other buildings still intact in this same general area are:-

130. Educational Ctr Class Room.

160.   Hobbies Centre.

180.   Library & Educ Flt Office.

The Bank and Post Office are still across the road from Station HQ in building and there are some new shops in this area.

Radio Gan Studio

As a pioneer of Radio Gan and having the privilege of being the first announcer and disc jockey, I was particularly interested in seeing if there was anything left of the old station. In 1960 the original Radio Gan studio and control room were situated in the Message Centre and 6SU Workshop, but I understand that, due to transmission security problems, the station was moved to building just to the rear of the Airport Control Tower.

We looked for this building but could not find it. In the end we resorted to asking a tower security guard where it was. He gladly escorted us and showed us some old foundations. They, unfortunately, are all that is left of the old station. I was now even more intrigued to know if the old Message Centre was standing and if the original Radio Gan rooms were in existence.

As the area all around the airport Control Tower is subject to personnel security restrictions the guard agreed to accompany us on our mission. We gained the impression that all the security guards on Gan had very little to do as the tourists visiting the island were always well behaved, very few locals visited the island, and there were a maximum of two flights a day to cause them any other problems. Our guard was very happy to show us around and brighten up, what to him would have been, another fairly boring day.

We were soon passing the Crash Rescue Tender Building (ref. 73), which although in the same place, had been rebuilt. Next to it was the Fire Section Garage (ref. 70) not rebuilt, and with all the original internal RAF signs intact. Then, there we were, looking at the old Message Centre almost exactly as I remembered it. We soon located the two rooms that used to house Radio Gan but unfortunately could not enter them as someone was now living there and washing was festooned on a line just outside the rooms. I took some pictures and we moved on. Building 133, GRSS/6SUEng Cord Flt, no longer exists although the foundations were still visible.

During our walk back to the main road we made positive identification of the following buildings but have no idea what they are being used for now:

Female Transients Quarters

Aircrews Quarters

Single Airmen's Quarters.

VIP Quarters.

Static Water Tank. With Water.

One building that we did see every time we left or returned to the hotel was number 38 the Bedding Store. This building still stands in grand isolation and is now a tourist trinket and goody shop.

It was now Sunday 11th October and our holiday was all too quickly coming to an end. We lazed around the pool in the morning and after lunch decided to walk up the beach to the old oil jetty. It was a sunny day with little breeze and the water was crystal clear. We walked out onto the oil jetty taking care to negotiate the holes left in the walkway where the steel treadplates had been removed. Now we were close to the 9-inch, spun-iron oil pipes we could see just how much they had deteriorated. They were all very rusty and had corroded right through the metal in very many places leaving gapping holes. We walked to the Oil Tanker discharge point at the end of the jetty and here found disconnected pipes and parts of the original pipe system missing altogether.

Two local Maldivians who had brought their fishing lines with them joined us on the jetty and they soon set about casting out over the reef edge. They did not catch anything whilst we were there and we returned slowly along the jetty looking down through the crystal clear water at the fish below. There seemed to be a large number of Garfish in the water as well as Parrot and Blue Surgeon fish and we stopped, filmed and watched them for some time.

Back at the hotel more visitors had arrived on the morning's flight. We had heard that there had been serious delays at Male because of problems with the Dash 7 aircraft and a back up Dornier aircraft with just 16 seats had been used to ferry in the new guests.

After lunch we returned to the sun beds around the poolside and here we met two of the new arrivals, Brian Underhill and his wife from Grimsby in the UK. Brian was an ex-RAF Ganite and was on the island in the 1960s as a Fireman. We were soon chatting about the old times and looking at the many photographs he had brought with him. Brian had also come to see one of the Maldivian boys whom he had kept in touch with since completing his year on Gan.

Unfortunately Brian and his wife's stay on Gan was now limited to just three days due to the aircraft delays in Male. We exchanged addresses and agreed to keep in touch.

It was now Monday 12th October and Diane had been totally bitten with the snorkelling bug. We therefore decided to go snorkelling just east of the oil jetty in the morning and west of the main Gan jetty in the afternoon. Although the sun was shining brightly and it was very hot, a stiff breeze was stirring up the waters, and the crystal clear conditions of the previous day had gone. We spent about an hour in the waters by the oil jetty, saw just a few fish, and came across a very large steel chain heavily encrusted with coral. I believe that this chain was probably one of those used to support the submarine nets across the Gan channel during the war as it disappeared out and down the side of the reef. We also looked for the two landing craft that we were informed had been sunk in this area but it was difficult to see anything in the cloudy water and we saw no sign of them.

After lunch we made our way to the beach west of the Maldivian jetty and after a suitable period of rest in the beach chairs thoughtfully provided by the hotel we returned to snorkelling again. The water on the reef edge was now much clearer and we spent the whole afternoon lazily making our way up and down the reef watching the fish feeding, fighting territorial battles or just swimming around in shoals. This must be one of the world's most relaxing pastimes.

The last day of our holiday on Gan, Tuesday 13th October, had arrived and we went for breakfast around 0900 hours as usual. We arrived at our usual table and found that it was decorated across one corner with a great profusion of multicoloured tropical flowers. It was all beautifully arranged and we thanked our waiter very much. He had obviously spent a considerable time making the display of flowers look just right. Other tables were also sporting brilliant displays of flowers so we knew the guests at these tables would be on the same late afternoon flight as us.

We had done most of our packing the previous evening so decided that we would once again borrow the bikes and ride across and take a closer look at the Maldivian Mosque at the site of the old Pakistani Camp. The skies were overcast and there were dark threatening clouds on the horizon. We soon arrived at the Mosque and met a Maldivian gentleman on the road outside who was busy sweeping leaves and fir needles from the road. We asked him if we could have a look at the Mosque and take some pictures. He immediately asked if I was ex RAF? We were soon deep in conversation about the good old times. He spoke excellent English and had worked, like many of his friends, for the RAF a number of years. He readily agreed to our request to take pictures but asked if we could limit these to outside the building.

The Mosque itself is well maintained, as are the grounds and graveyard around it. We noted one of the gravel pathways was being relayed and there were small piles of gravel around waiting to be spread. This gravel must have been imported from outside the Maldives since only coral sand and chipping's can be found locally. Outside the entrance of the Mosque was a well providing water for the worshippers and an area set-aside for their shoes.

We were soon waving goodbye to our Maldivian friend who had been joined by his colleague who was working on the gravel path. Threatening clouds had been gathering all day and we had only arrived back at the hotel a few minutes before it began raining. It rained as only it can in the tropics and showed no sign of stopping. We made a mad dash from our room to the hotel at lunchtime and found that our table now had further decoration. Spelt out in multicolour grains of rice was the word 'Goodbye'. Our attentive waiter had been busy yet again. We were very sorry we had to leave and thanked him sincerely for helping to make our holiday so enjoyable.

Everyone leaving gathered in the reception area of the hotel about 1630 hours, settled their accounts and sat down to await the bus. Emmanuella arrived to tell us that there would be a short delay due to the "late arrival of the incoming aircraft". Now where have I heard that before? What she failed to tell us was that the aircraft had not taken off from Male yet! The manager also appeared and offered everyone free drinks for which we were all very grateful. At least it had now stopped raining and the sun was attempting to break through again. Time passed slowly and we were eventually informed that the aircraft had departed from Male just before 1800 hours. With 1½ hours flying time that would mean landing at 1930 hours on Gan at the earliest.

The manager of the Ocean Reef was very understanding at our frustration at having to wait so long and organised the restaurant to open at 1930 hours for a complementary dinner. Our waiter was soon serving us again not having expected to see us quite so soon. Eventually, during our meal, we heard the aircraft arrive and we were soon all packed into the bus and being driven to the airport. Our luggage had all been taken earlier. Formalities at the terminal building were kept to a minimum although a thorough search of our hand baggage was carried out by the security guards.

We were soon airborne in the Dash 7 on route for Male for our onward flight on Emirates Airlines to Dubai where we were to stop with friends for seven days. This was going to be the 'shopping' part of our holiday but I was so relaxed after our ten days in the Addoo Atoll it was not going to worry me at all...

General Observations

I believe it would be remiss of me if I did not make some general comments relating to the Hotel, Addoo Atoll and Gan in particular.

The Gan/Feydhoo causeway

This is a well-constructed, well-used and welcome addition, aiding transportation in the Addoo Atoll. Now it has been equipped with pipes routing water from sea to lagoon sides of the islands it can no longer be criticised as a potential environmental hazard. The causeway also serves as one side of a natural harbour for small yachts and marine craft. It may be remembered by ex RAF personnel that just off the north west point of Gan, and very near the old Officers' Mess, there is a natural channel in the reef some 40 feet deep and 20 feet wide. This allows relatively easy access for boats into this area of water with the northern boundary of the "harbour" being the lagoon reef itself and the east and west boundaries being the two islands.

Addoo Atoll Waste

Addoo Atoll has a major waste problem that is not only spoiling the islands and beaches but is also posing the threat of environmental pollution.

It is quite understandable that those living in these islands for many years have needed to get rid of their rubbish. For many years when these islanders were effectively living in isolation then to throw unwanted items into the sea was a logical thing to do. Such items thrown away would almost have certainly been made of natural items such as wood or palm branch leaves. Such items being naturally degradable. When the call of nature came to islanders then a visit to the waters edge of any beach resulted in swift removal of offending items by the tide.

Unfortunately, with the arrival of so-called 'modern civilisation' to these islands, has come the problem of disposing of man-made items such as plastic bottles, plastic wrapping and packing materials, as well as cans and glass bottles. None of these items are biodegradable but are being disposed of in the same way that waste items were disposed of in bygone years.

Throughout the islands we saw evidence of indiscriminate rubbish dumping in all manner of places. Even right up at Koattey in northern Hithadhoo we saw piles of rubbish dumped amongst the bushes by the roadside. It wasn't quite as bad on Gan since here they have a centralised dump for waste away from the main areas of accommodation.

The establishment of an effective sewage disposal system on Gan was a priority when work began to establish the RAF's Staging Post in 1956. This was no easy task for the designers and planners of the system due to the fact that the highest point on Gan was no more than five feet above the highest sea level. This meant that the whole system had to be pumped for effective disposal of the effluent from underground septic tanks to a point well out to sea beyond the outer reef. Such a method of disposal was, and perhaps still is, acceptable due to the relatively small number of people resident on Gan at any one time and that effluent is being dumped into some of the very deepest seas in the world.

It is understood that similar sewage systems are now installed on other islands in the Addoo Atoll for use by the general population. However, obviously old habits die hard, and on Feydhoo we witnessed first-hand older brothers and sisters taking younger members of the family to the water's edge to relieve themselves. It will obviously take a long time to bring about the necessary change in the culture and habits of some of the population.

It was good to see that the waste problem is obviously one that both central and local Government is aware of and we saw a number of posters on the islands indicating to locals and visitors alike to "dispose of litter carefully". I believe that if the Government is really serious about doing something about the waste problem then they must be willing to spend more money to organise, and pay for, the regular collection of waste on all the islands and to find an acceptable method for its disposal. None of the islands is large enough for land dump sites to be established and these would soon attract world wide attention from environmental groups. It is a major problem that requires resolving as quickly as possible. Perhaps one of the most effective places to start is in the schools by teaching the children about the dangers of environmental pollution. There are many examples world wide that they could learn from. They certainly live in some of the most beautiful islands in the world that must be preserved for the enjoyment of generations to come.

Television in Addoo Atoll

We had noted throughout the Atoll that many of the houses appeared to have television sets but very few houses had satellite dishes outside the homes to receive TV signals. We found out later that there is no direct TV service available in the Southern Maldive islands, but there are a considerable number of video hire shops that are very well stocked and used. Those people who are lucky enough to have satellite dishes can receive TV broadcasts originating from the UK as well as from America, for example, CNN. A government-run Television and Radio service on Male broadcasts regular news and entertainment programmes. There are no Independent broadcasters.

Ocean Reef Club Hotel Catering

From the first day of our stay in the hotel we found the standard of catering good. Meals are fairly simple reflecting the local environment and fish based dishes nearly always made a daily appearance in one guise or another. As someone who is not a great fish lover I was pleasantly surprised. Perhaps that was so because here the fish is always fresh and it has been the staple diet of these islanders for many many years. The hotel cooks certainly knew how to make such dishes appetising.

Breakfast

At Breakfast time you served yourself from a well-spread table and a chef was on hand to cook eggs in any way you liked them. The eggs were always fresh and could be served poached, boiled, fried or scrambled. If preferred, a plain or mixed omelette could be conjured up. Various cereals were always available but it should be remembered that all milk is the long-life type and may not suit everyone's taste. There was always a selection of fruit juices on the table and locally-made croissants were usually available as well as a variety of jams.

When first arriving for breakfast you would be asked if you would like tea or coffee and by the time you had selected your meal and returned to your table your drink was there together with hot toast. Tea or coffee was on tap and your waiter would top your cup up as required. Additional toast could also be requested.

Lunch

Lunch was an integral part of our holiday package and if ever we return to the hotel then we may well choose the 'bed, breakfast and evening meal' option, especially as toasted sandwiches and other appetising snacks were available from the coffee shop throughout the day. Again the food served at lunchtime was good and more than adequate to meet anyone's needs. Soup, then a variety of both fish and meat dishes were served during our holiday with both fresh and tinned fruit being available for dessert.

Dinner

Dinner was available in the restaurant from 20:00 hours and that gave plenty of time to visit the bar, relax and have a drink beforehand. We found one particular barman to be most efficient. Once he knew your tipple he would have drinks on your table almost before you had reached the lounge chairs to sit down. If you required a top-up, then all that was needed was a nod in his direction.

A selection of red and white wines was always available to go with the meal but these were quite expensive and the choice somewhat limited. Wines do not keep well in this tropical climate.

Bottled water could always be ordered at the table and if you did not finish your bottle then it would be marked and returned to your table at the next meal, unfortunately not chilled.

A starter such as soup or fruit juice preceded all meals. The main courses served were from a variety of fish and meat and some were curried. There was usually a variety of vegetables available or a fresh salad with tomatoes, shredded cabbage and carrots and locally grown cucumber. At least twice, during our ten-day holiday, dinner was served as a barbecue outside around the pool area under the stars with tables being lit with candles.

We found all our meals adequate and carefully served by our smart, very attentive, but unobtrusive, waiter, but if you are expecting *haute cuisine* food served by flunky waiters in penguin suits then forget having a holiday here.

Our waiter told us that he normally left Maradhoo for Gan at 0530 hours each morning and sometimes did not leave to return home at night until all the dinner guests had left the restaurant, or barbecue, as late as 2330 hours at night. He certainly worked a very long day and was at times required to return in the middle of the night to serve meals to guests who had arrived late due to plane delays. His wife was a local health worker on Maradhoo and was very understanding about his situation. His service to us throughout our holiday was 100%.

The Maldivian People

Wherever we travelled in the Addoo Atoll we were given a warm welcome by the local Maldivian population. They are a very gentle and peace-loving nation. Islam is the national religion and all Maldivians are Sunni Muslims. Not once during our stay did we hear adults or children raising their voices in anger or arguing amongst themselves. Gardeners, waiters, boatmen, managers and all hotel staff were there to help you enjoy your holiday in the most relaxing way possible. All the security Guards we met were quite happy to escort you wherever you wished to go and "No you cannot" was never heard. One example of the extraordinary lengths that local people would go to make you feel welcome was amply demonstrated by the Maldivian lady who made up our hotel room each day.

On returning to our room after our first days holiday we found the room well tidied, the bathroom spotless and the clothes and shoes we had left out, now put away tidily. The bed had been made-up and made to look even more attractive by circular hand-pleating of the top sheet. A Frangipani flower placed at the centre of the pleating topped this off. This was all very simple, but very attractive.

Returning to our room each evening we found the complexity of the pleating of our bed sheets and the amount and variety of flowers left in the room increased. The ultimate decoration occurred on the seventh day of our holiday when Frangipani, Hibiscus and many other tropical flowers adorned our bed, furniture and room in great profusion. We were sure that our lady had not been told to decorate our room and had done so purely to please us. It certainly made our holiday very memorable.

Sea levels

Since my RAF days on Gan a sea defence wall has been built along the lagoon shoreline from the main jetty, out and around the north-east point of Gan, by the old Officers Mess, and up to the new causeway. It then extends further on past the Swimming Pagar towards the runway intersection. Similarly at the eastern end of the island new sea defence walls have been built. Many of the coral sand beaches around the island that I remember from 1960 no longer exist and although it is a very subjective assessment, I believe the seas around Gan are now noticeably deeper. I have reached this conclusion based on the amount of coral beach that is now exposed at low tide.

Shops

Now that the NAAFI is no longer resident on Gan, a number of shops have come into being. These reflect the requirements of the residents on Gan, especially the Sri Lankan factory workers, as well as the passing tourist trade. Some sell everything from shoes to radios, films to hair spray, whilst others specialise in cheap goods to catch the tourist's eye. There are one or two shops that sell local produce and hand-made Maldivian goods and some that sell goods for the home. One shop near the old Airmen's mess sold electrical fittings, car and motorbike spares, plumbing fitting, tins and tubs of food, cloth, postcards and many other items. What impressed us was that packs of margarine were neatly stacked alongside gasket sets for cars and motorbikes. All the stock was well mixed. Shopkeepers always made us very welcome and were not worried if you did not buy anything before leaving.

The Coral Reef

One of the biggest disappointments as far as I was concerned was to find approximately 90% of the coral reefs in the Addoo Atoll were now dead. When I left Gan in 1960 I would estimate that at least 95% of the reefs were living, with a good mix of hard and soft corals. At no time during our holiday in 1998 did we see any soft corals. There were sea anemones and clams and the fish were still there in great profusion, but the coral was badly damaged.

There has been much speculation in the press recently as to why coral reefs are dying. This is not just a problem affecting the Maldives. Reefs in other areas in the Seychelles, Mauritius and in the Western Pacific from Vietnam to the Philippines and Indonesia have all died or been bleached. This has occurred because the coral has been starved of the symbiotic algae which is the coral's food and energy source. The only marine areas in the world that appear to have escaped this devastation are the atolls of the Central Pacific.

Nearly all this damage has occurred over the last two years as a direct result of an unprecedented rise in sea temperatures that are now at record levels. This temperature rise can be attributed directly to general global warming which has also caused an increase in sea levels. We can only hope that the symbiotic algae will soon adapt to living in the warmer seas and today's devastated coral reefs around the world will be able to return to their former glory.

1998. A selection of reef fish (below).

Empress Angelfish.

Blue Surgeonfish.

1998. The Astra Cinema (above) and Memorial Garden (below).

1998. The Message Centre (above) and The Gan Jetty (below).

1998. Former Station HQ (above) and former Billet 47 (below).

1998. The new Causeway (above) and former Radio Gan studio (below).

1998. The new Harbour (above) and former Guardhouse (below).

1998. Cemetary (above) and The Gan Power Station (below).

1998. The VIP Centre (above) and former billets, now hotel chalets (below).

1998. Hotel chalet (above). Chalet bedroom beautifully presented (left) and the Hotel reception and shop (below).

1998. Former oil jetty (above) former Airmen's Club (below).

1998. Former Bedding Store (above); Ocean Reef Approach Road (below).

1998. Hithadhoo Pharmacy.

1998. Maldivian schoolchildren.

1998. Maldivian-style barbecue amongst the palm trees.

1998. Fresh Tuna on sale (above); fishing boat under construction (below).

1998. Safari boat under construction.

Gan 1998
Picturesque views of the beach at Viligili (above)
and the coral Lagoon (below).

Endnote

I hope that those of you who have managed to 'stay the course' and read all of my book have found it of some interest, especially if you are a former 'Gannite'. I have tried to be as factual as possible and where I could I have checked such facts from independent sources. Any comments made are mine and mine alone and I hope I have not offended anyone.

Our 1998 holiday on the island helped to answer many of the questions that had built up in my mind over the 38 years since leaving Gan in December 1960. I hope my descriptions will answer some of your questions too. I still however have a strong desire to return again with my wife to explore the islands still further. If any reader of these words visits the Addoo Atoll sometime in the future then I would welcome a note from you, however large or small, about your visit.

Thank you for your patience,

Happy Holidays and Best Wishes

Michael Butler
June, 2001